BEFRIEND YOUR BRAIN

A YOUNG PERSON'S GUIDE TO DEALING WITH ANY~~~~~~~~~~~N, FREAK-OUTS,

FAITH G HARPER PhD, LPC-S, ACS, ACN

MICROCOSM PUBLISHING
PORTLAND, OR

BEFRIEND YOUR BRAIN
A Young Person's Guide to Dealing with Anxiety, Depression, Freak-outs, and Triggers

Part of the 5 Minute Therapy Series

© Faith G Harper, 2021, 2023
This edition © Microcosm Publishing, 2021
Second Printing, 2023
ISBN 9781648410383
This is Microcosm #268

For a catalog, write or visit:
Microcosm Publishing
2752 N Williams Ave.
Portland, OR 97227
(503)799-2698
www.Microcosm.Pub/**BEFRIEND**

LIBRARY OF CONGRESS CATALOGING-IN-PUBLICATION DATA

Names: Harper, Faith G., author.
Title: Befriend your brain : using science to get over anxiety, depression, anger, freak-outs, and triggers / Faith G. Harper, PhD, LPC-S, ACS.
Other titles: Unfuck your brain
Description: Portland, OR : Microcosm Publishing, [2021] | Originally published in 2017 as: Un***k your brain : using science to get over anxiety, depression, anger, freak-outs, and triggers. | Includes bibliographical references. | Summary: "Do you freak out at small things? Do you yell at people or things when you don't mean to? Do you sometime cry or get scared and you aren't sure why? Does it sometimes feel like your feelings control you? All of these feelings are a normal part of life for everybody but sometimes they're just too much and it seems like you're the only one the planet that feels them. Our brains are doing their best to help us out, but sometimes we get hurt instead. And sometimes we hurt people we love, too, because we just don't know what to do with all of our feelings. With humor and patience, Dr. Faith G. Harper shows you the science behind why your brain is acting up and ideas for new ways to respond when you're feeling scared, sad, anxious, or angry. You can train your brain to be your friend and help you live a happy, calm, and healthy life. If you have experienced trauma or if you have a hard time feeling good and getting along with other people, this book can help. This is an adaptation of Dr. Faith's bestselling book (which has an R-rated title), written for tweens, teens, and the adults trying to help them navigate it all"-- Provided by publisher.
Identifiers: LCCN 2021037347 | ISBN 9781648410383 (trade paperback)
Subjects: LCSH: Psychic trauma--Treatment--Popular works. | Stress management. | Mental health. | Psychotherapy.
Classification: LCC RC552.T7 H365 2021 | DDC 616.85/21--dc23
LC record available at https://lccn.loc.gov/2021037347

MICROCOSM·PUBLISHING

MICROCOSM PUBLISHING is Portland's most diversified publishing house and distributor with a focus on the colorful, authentic, and empowering. Our books and zines have put your power in your hands since 1996, equipping readers to make positive changes in their lives and in the world around them. Microcosm emphasizes skill-building, showing hidden histories, and fostering creativity through challenging conventional publishing wisdom with books and bookettes about DIY skills, food, bicycling, gender, self-care, and social justice. What was once a distro and record label was started by Joe Biel in a bedroom and has become among the oldest independent publishing houses in Portland, OR. We are a politically moderate, centrist publisher in a world that has inched to the right for the past 80 years.

CONTENTS

PREFACE

First of all, no one expected the original version of this book to be as hugely popular as it was. I'm a nobody from San Antonio, Texas, and I wrote a book published by a medium-sized publisher that appeals to punks and weirdos (my people!). And it didn't get popular because Oprah found it. It got popular because those same punks and weirdos read it and passed it to their friends. Who passed it on and passed it on and passed it on. And a couple of years after it was published, it ended up on best-seller lists (which goes to show that punks and weirdos can absolutely change the world).

And I got tons and tons of fan mail. Most of it was about how helpful they found the book and how they loved that I write the same way that I talk. The other one percent hated my language and thought it was disrespectful of my academic background. I guess if I have a PhD I should sound boring and stodgy? They demanded a "clean" version of the book because they didn't like my language.

My publisher shrugged and said, "When you try to make everyone happy you end up making no one happy. You sound like yourself, and that's what makes the book good."

Then we got a note from someone who worked with teens with significant trauma history who were also involved in the justice system. Which is a lot of crap to go through before legal adulthood. She used my books regularly, especially the original brain book, and had to black out the f-bombs. She asked if we had considered making a kid-friendly version. Not dumbing down the science or anything, but something that could be used in schools and detention centers and the like without needing to use a sharpie every other word.

So, here's the thing.

Not only do punks and weirdos change the world as a group, one person with a reasonable and respectful request can also change the world. She wasn't yelling about how I write, she just wanted to use it in places where it was really needed. I sent that email to my publisher who said, "That's totally fair, we should do it!"

So this book, the "kid friendly" version, was officially approved.

So the next question was, do we have someone else write it, or do I do it? Of course I wanted to do it! I did not want someone else dumbing everything down. I work with a lot of teens and preteens in my private practice, and they are incredibly smart and thoughtful.

One of my biggest complaints about mental health books written for people under eighteen is that they treat readers like they're dumb. And I've found y'all tend to be more self-aware and world-aware that most of the middle-aged people I know. And y'all are the ones who'll be fixing this planet after we are long gone.

So no talking down or dumbing down of *anything*. No cheesy. No fake positives and cheer. Just real life science, help, and advice. Because you're already living real life, and you already have real problems.

Let's get to it.

INTRODUCTION

How do our brains become a problem? Let us count the ways.

Maybe you're stressed out or overwhelmed. Maybe really sad or really angry. Maybe you've lost someone important to you. Maybe you suspect that you're struggling with depression or anxiety. Maybe you have been using really unhealthy coping skills to deal with all of it.

Maybe a lot of those things. Maybe all of them.

And then feeling messed up becomes a vicious cycle. We feel weird and crazy for feeling weird and crazy. We feel like we are weak. Or broken. Or fundamentally flawed. And *that* is the most helpless feeling in the world. Fundamentally flawed means un-fixable. So why bother trying?

But guess what? These things—anger, depression, anxiety, the rest of it—are **adaptive strategies**, which are *anything your body uses to react to and move through change*. If you don't believe anything else I have to say, I hope you believe this part. These feelings are normal. We're wired for self-protection and survival, and that's exactly what your brain is doing when it's acting like it forgot how to work right. It's actually doing its job, which is to protect you!

So much of what we call mental illness is really a case of brain chemicals gone haywire. And most of this comes from the stressful and traumatic life events we cope with. Our brains may be responding to big, life-altering traumatic experiences ... *but not always*. The trouble may also lie in our day-to-day relationships and interactions ... the small ways people push our buttons, violate our boundaries, and disrespect our need for safety. And for most people? It's a hot mess combination of the three.

What if you could understand where all of those thoughts and feelings are coming from? We are way more likely to get better if we know *why* we are having a certain problem rather than just focusing on the symptoms. If we treat stress, anxiety, or depression, for example, without looking at some of the *causes* of the stress, anxiety, and depression, then we aren't doing everything we can to make things ACTUALLY BETTER.

It's like if you get a rash (bear with me, gross analogy, I know). You can treat the rash and maybe even make it go away, but if you don't figure out what you were allergic to? Continued issues with rashes are pretty likely.

Same with the brain. If you can understand better why you are doing, thinking, and feeling the things you are doing, thinking, and feeling, the getting-better part gets way easier. And it doesn't have to be explained in a super-complicated fancy-pants way to make sense and be us eful. Basically, **trauma** *is anything that overwhelms our ability to cope*. And if we don't have a chance to heal, trauma can cause more and more issues even years later. So this book is all about understanding the how-and-why with enough detail to help you do the healing part now. Because you aren't fundamentally broken and stuck like this forever.

WHO IS THIS BOOK FOR?

This book is for the people who ask, *"But, WHY?"* all the time. The people who annoyed the crap out of the adults around them when they were little kids by asking all the questions about how the world worked because the *why* is REALLY NEEDFUL INFORMATION.

This book is for all the people who hate being told what to do by other people. Who just want the tools and the information they need to figure out what to do for *themselves*. You may be figuring this out by yourself or with a rock-star therapist (or another adult you trust) who treats you like a fully functional human who doesn't need bossing around. In any case, you know you are in charge of your own life when it comes down to it, because no matter how old you are, you're still responsible for all the consequences.

This book is for everyone who is tired of hearing (or thinking) that they are just crazy. Or stupid. Or lazy. Or "too sensitive." Or just need to "get over" themselves. Who are tired of feeling bad but even more tired of other people thinking they *enjoy* feeling bad. Like anyone would choose misery. Like they think that if you could figure out why you were miserable you wouldn't do something about it. Of course you would. So this book is about *why* you are miserable so you *can* do something about it.

WHAT IS GOING TO HAPPEN IN THIS BOOK?

So, okay. You're thinking: *That's all well and good, fancy doctor lady. How is this book going to help? What makes this book all kinds of special and different from the eleventy-billion other self-help books out there? I'm skeptical, tbh.*

Word. You should be. My shelves are crammed full of books that I would like to demand a time refund for.

This book is different, for serious.

First up? I'm gonna lay some science on you. Not complex, dry, boring-as-a-box-of-rocks science but *"Ah, okay, that makes sense, how come no one ever explained it to me like that before???"* science. It doesn't take twelve years of college and two hundred thousand dollars of student loan debt to understand any of this. I can generally explain what you need to know in about five to ten minutes (or an equivalent number of written pages, as the case may be).

Second? I'm not gonna lay all this brain science on you and then say, "Yeah, sorry about that" and walk away. I'm going to go through a lot of advice that is actually practical and doable for getting better. Because you know what? The situation isn't hopeless. You aren't hopeless. GETTING BETTER HAPPENS.

Third? I'm going to go through a lot of the treatment options out there. I'm not against medication and Western care ... but I do believe they belong in their proper place as one of *many* treatment options. All **holistic care** means is *care for the whole person*. And we have to build a plan that works for us.

For example, my best line of defense is eating healthy, being forced to exercise now and then, taking herbal supplements, and embracing acupuncture, meditation, massage, and pedicures as part of my wellness regime.

And I will fight anyone *to the pain* (yes, *The Princess Bride* reference[1]) over my belief that pedicures are therapeutic. For my son, it's football, weightlifting, grounding exercises, meditation, a highly structured school environment, neurofeedback, and a combo of both supplements and Western meds. We all have unique needs. Pedicures, strangely, are not on his list.

And throughout the book there will be mini-exercises that will help you process the work that you are doing. It's not homework; you don't have to pass a final exam. But having ways to process all the stuff that may come up for you is important.

TAKE ACTION: TAKING YOUR OWN TEMPERATURE

How often in life have you been given permission to feel what you feel? Rarely to never is my bet.

We are generally told not to feel negative emotions. We're told they are bad and to be avoided.

And we're going to go further into why that is the exact opposite of how to get better.

But in the meantime, it can be really helpful to tap into what you're feeling. Take your own temperature, so to speak. And have an action plan for if it gets too high. Later in this book, you will learn more exercises that you can incorporate. But let's start with the simplest first.

Shut your eyes right now and notice:

- What's going on in your body? Like does your stomach hurt? Your chest feel tight? Your breathing acting weird? Are you curled up in a ball in the corner?

- What are you thinking? (It may not be actual thoughts but flashes of memory tapes playing.)

- What are you feeling in response to that? Name those emotions. Rate the severity of them (mild, medium, strong, off the charts). Some possible emotions on the next page.

- And, seriously, what other things are you dealing with in your everyday life that are either helping you cope or making it worse?

joyful EXCITED

Cheerful satisfied

FRUSTRATED COZY

angry CALM

Sad Despairing

Amused SURPRISED

confused nervous

ANNOYED **Worried**

This exercise might be really hard for you. Lots of people have no clue how they feel. That's okay, too. You've been trained to disconnect and push aside your feelings. Told what you feel is wrong. Not allowed to experience them.

So if you don't know ... acknowledge that, too. You may find as you do this particular exercise over time, you will start connecting to what you feel. Not knowing does *not* make you a self-help book dropout. It's just more vital information about where you are right now.

All this exercise does is give you back your power to own what is going on inside you.

Forgetting your past isn't possible, but it doesn't mean you have to keep living there. And that starts with knowing this: *you are completely allowed to feel what you feel.*

PART ONE

THIS IS YOUR BRAIN ON TRAUMA

CHAPTER ONE
WHEN DID MY BRAIN TURN AGAINST ME?

As I said before, things like anxiety, depression, addiction, and anger issues are part of the whole complicated process of your brain responding to everything you've gone through. The brain is really just trying to do its job by protecting you the best way it knows how, but it often ends up being part of the problem in the long run. It's like your friend that offers to beat up anyone who upsets you. Maybe that feels good at first, but it just gets everyone into trouble in the long run. Life is hard, and other people can suck sometimes. It might not be a traumatic experience that gets in the way of moving forward and living life. There are plenty of things that aren't full-blown traumas ... but are definitely not kittens, rainbows, and teddy bears either. Like with trauma, the coping skills we create for *these* situations tend to be less and less useful over time—and downright exhausting.

The good news is, no matter how long you've been stuck in this quicksand, you can rewire your response and make friends with your brain.

WHY IS MY BRAIN A BIG, HOT MESS?

We have a tendency to separate mental health from physical health. As if they don't affect each other in a continuous feedback loop or something.

Stuff we learn about the brain itself generally falls under the "physical health" category. Thoughts, feelings, and behaviors fall under the "mental health" category.

So where does this thinking and feeling fit in our body? Our mind seems to be a helium balloon floating over our heads at all times. We are holding on to the string, maybe, but it isn't really part of us (though we are still held accountable for all of it).

That image of a disembodied brain isn't helpful. It doesn't make one bit of sense.

And what we actually know about the brain is this: it at least somewhat lives in our *gut*. Unique microorganisms reside in our gut (our digestive system) and communicate so consistently with our actual brains (through the gut-brain axis . . . an actual real thing) that they are referred to as a second brain, one that plays a huge role in guiding our emotions. Ever had a gut reaction? Like you *knew* something bad was about to happen? What about an upset stomach after something bad happened? Yeah, that's a real thing.

Which is to say, instead of being a thing that's barely tethered to us and gets us in trouble all the time, our mind actually lies deep in the middle of our body, acting as a control center, taking in tons of information, and making decisions before we are even aware that a decision needs to be made.

It bears repeating: our thoughts, feelings, and behaviors are rooted deep in our physical bodies, which affect how our brains perceive the world around us, based on past experiences and current information. So it might be the understatement of the decade to say that knowing what's going on in your brain and how all that works is HUGE. If all is bopping along and the landing is smooth, we don't notice

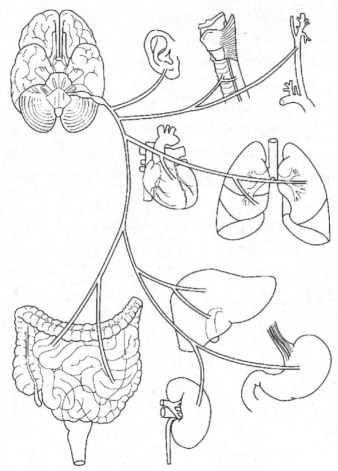

The vagus nerve relays information throughout the body, both to and from the brain.

any problems. But when we have a rough landing? When brain-traffic control doesn't manage its traffic patterns properly, we see the effects:

- Freaking out
- Avoiding anything important that we need to take care of
- Feeling upset and angry and frustrated all the time
- Being rude or nasty or hurtful to people we care about
- Putting stuff in our bodies that we know isn't good for us
- Doing things we know are dumb or pointless or destructive

None of these things are helpful. But they all make sense. They are examples of our brains trying to feel back in control. Which means that, while they aren't actually helpful responses, they are responses that make sense.

As we navigate the world, bad things happen. The brain stores info about anything bad as a giant DANGER sign in order to avoid that bad thing happening again. Your brain has adapted to the circumstances in your life and started doing things to protect you, bless it. Sometimes these responses are helpful. Sometimes the responses, like the ones I just mentioned above, become a bigger problem than the *actual* problem was. Your brain isn't *trying* to make life more difficult for you (even though sometimes it totally does).

And even if you aren't dealing with a specific trauma? Messed up coping skills, bad habits, and funky behaviors all wire in similar ways. Research is showing that these issues are actually some of the easier ones to treat in therapy ... if we address what's really going on, rather than just the symptoms.

One of the most helpful things I do as a therapist is explain what is going on inside the brain and how the work we do in therapy is designed to rewire our responses to certain situations. Lemme explain what I mean by that.

BRAIN 101

If any part of the book is complicated, it's this part. Because brains are pretty complicated so hang with me, we got this.

The prefrontal cortex (we'll call it the PFC), essentially the front part of your brain, is the part in

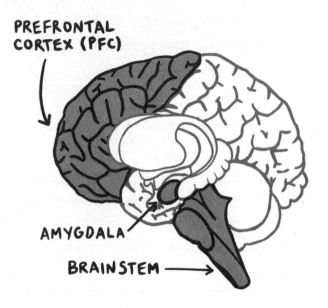

PREFRONTAL CORTEX (PFC)

AMYGDALA

BRAINSTEM

charge of **executive functioning**, which includes *problem-solving, goal-oriented behaviors, and managing social interactions.* Essentially, executive function is just straight-up *thinking.*

The PFC is also the part that takes the longest to develop as we grow up. It isn't at full capacity until we are in our mid-twenties. That doesn't mean that it doesn't exist in children, adolescents, and young adults. And it sure doesn't mean you have a free pass on acting a fool if you are younger. But it does mean all our brain wiring creates new and more complex communication pathways as we get older and wiser.

And if it all goes well, the PFC continues to work better and better—a definite benefit of aging.

Hold on to that *if-it-all-goes-well* part for a minute, though.

So the PFC is the part that is theoretically in charge.

And the PFC is, understandably, highly connected to the rest of the brain. The ventral portion (which is just the backside of the PFC . . . the PFC booty, so to speak) is directly linked to an entirely different area of the brain . . . the part that stores emotions, and the entire PFC gets feedback from the brainstem arousal systems. More on these in a minute.

So whatever information is being sent to the PFC from these other parts of the brain impacts that whole thinking thing. There is a region of the PFC called the anterior cingulate cortex (definitely not a test on all these words, I swear) whose job is to manage the conversation between the PFC (think-y brain) and the limbic system (feel-y brain) and then make suggestions about whatever mess we are dealing with.

And our wiring in that area is *weird*. The brain cells here are called spindle neurons . . . they are long, leggy supermodels instead of short and bushy like they are everywhere else. And they are *fast*. They send signals way faster than the rest of the neurons, so you are hit up with an emotional response before you have a chance to think about what just happened.

Why those and why there? Only humans, great apes, and certain whales and dolphins have spindle neurons. A lot of scientists think that they are part of our evolution to higher cognition (flexible thinking, decision making, and self-control, for example).

And in order to think more, we have to feel more—and then take both into account when making decisions. Emotions are just as important for our survival as thoughts.

THE ANNOYING AMYGDALA

So that middle-ish part of the brain that I mentioned? The part doing the tango with the PFC booty? That's the limbic system. This portion is buried a bit in the folds of the brain, behind the PFC. If the PFC does the thinking part, the limbic system does the emotions part. And a lot of that emotions part has to do with how we store memories.

The amygdala and the hippocampus are two key parts of the limbic system, but most of what we now

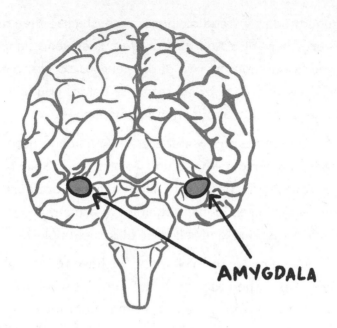

AMYGDALA

know about how trauma affects the brain is tied into research about the amygdala. The amygdala's job is to relate memories to emotions. But, to be more specific, the amygdala has been found to only store a *specific* kind of memory, not all of them.

The amygdala doesn't care one bit where you left your house key. The amygdala's function is to manage **episodic-autobiographical memory** (EAM). Essentially, this is *the storage of event-based knowledge*. Times, locations, people. Not your great-aunt's banana pudding recipe. Your stories about the world and how it works, especially anything bad or dangerous.

So why is this important? Episodic memories get stored as our individual survival maps that communicate with our amygdala about how we remember events and how crappy they made us feel. If something makes us really angry or scared or hurt or upset, our brain wants to help us avoid that happening again so the emotions and the memory become attached to each other like cat hair or static cling. So when we have an emotional response in the future, the amygdala immediately pulls up the memory file to go with it in order to decide how to respond.

What fires together, wires together.

Say you got flowers. Flowers are excellent, right? Even if you don't like flowers, they're not dangerous or anything ... if your past memories of getting flowers

were happy ones. Maybe someone you were into gave you flowers once. So when you're getting flowers in the future, seeing flowers, driving by a flower delivery truck? Nice feelings.

But say you got flowers when a loved one died . . . terribly and suddenly. Some nice person knew you were hurting and sent you flowers. But now even the *smell* of flowers makes you sick to your stomach.

The amygdala has turned the memory of flowers into an actual mnemonic for certain emotions. A **mnemonic** is just *a tool we use to help us remember important stuff*, like ROY G BIV to remember the colors of the rainbow or Every Good Boy Does Fine to remember the note breakdown on a musical scale. I've not been able to unlearn any of those mnemonics since elementary school, and that's been awhile. Mnemonics stick around.

The amygdala's job is to make sure you don't forget things that are very important. Remembering important-good is awesome. Nobody complains about nice memories. Remembering important-bad can be life saving—and can also really suck.

It sucks because the amygdala doesn't really distinguish super well between good and bad,

especially when it's trying to protect you. It ROY
G BIVs you into equating flowers with death. And
then you're walking down the street on a spring day
and smell the flowers blooming in your neighbor's
garden. And suddenly you feel like you've lost your
mind because even though your body is still in your
neighbor's garden, your brain is back at your loved
one's funeral. Nothing is actually wrong but, at the
same time, things are really, really bad all of a sudden.

FIGHT, FLIGHT, OR FREEZE . . . IT'S THE BRAINSTEM!

And that brings us to the last part of our brain convo,
where we talk about one final part of the brain . . . the
brainstem.

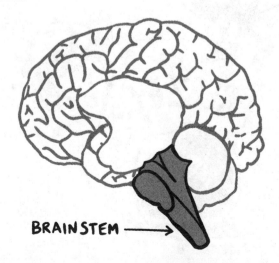

BRAINSTEM ⟶

The brainstem is the very base of the brain (makes sense, right?). It was the first part of the brain to even exist and the part that attaches to the vertebrae in our neck and back. The brain looks like a bunched up mass of overcooked pasta, right? This is the part of the brain that is starting to untangle itself from the rest of the noodles, straighten out a bit, and transition into being your spinal cord.

The brainstem is our fundamental survival tool. While heart muscles regulate basic needs like the

heart going *pump pump pump* all day long, the brainstem controls the rate, speed, and intensity of your heartbeat. So, instead of acting normal, it can, for example, ramp up for a panic attack. It's decided you need to pay attention because you might be dying. You know, the important stuff.

Being alert, being conscious, being aware of our surroundings? Brainstem tasks.

So when the brainstem is saying, "Danger Will Robinson!" or "OW OW OW," it is actually flooding the PFC with a bunch of **neurochemicals**, which are *any chemical substance that your body creates in order to convince your nervous system to react.* In this case, these neurochemicals are changing how the PFC operates.

The brainstem may be doing all the basic stuff, but it's also influencing how the rest of the brain acts.

When the brainstem senses danger, the behavioral actions of the PFC become *fight, flight, or freeze.*

Fight is BEAT THEM DOWN SO YOU CAN ESCAPE.

Flight is GET OUT OF HERE. THIS ISN'T SAFE.

And freeze is IF YOU CURL UP INTO A small ball AND DON'T RESPOND AT ALL MAYBE ALL THIS WILL GO AWAY.

Don't get me wrong ... these are essential survival tasks when something dangerous is going on. They are *crazy important* to our survival. This whole process is our emergency broadcast system.

The PFC takes in some outside information. The amygdala yells, "I remember that! Last time that happened, it hurt! Hurt sucks!" And the brainstem tells the PFC, "Get out of there! We don't like to hurt!"

So we say, "Peace out, threatening situation, gotta jet!" Or we fight back. Or we freeze up and play dead and hope the situation passes us over. All kinds of things can feel threatening ... like a final exam, or a work deadline, or a crowded grocery store. But those don't need an I NEED TO GET OUT BEFORE I BECOME A DINOSAUR SNACK response. Except the brainstem evolved to avoid being a dinosaur snack and *not* to deal with crowds, and traffic, and people who hit the heels of our feet with their shopping carts at the grocery store (you could totally argue the point that they are worse than hungry dinosaurs), so sometimes it *thinks* that annoying cart is a dino, or at least a real threat.

SQUISH IT ALL TOGETHER? WE GOT STORYTELLING BRAINS

We all understand this to a certain extent. The idea that human beings tell stories, that is. But only to a certain extent. Because we don't really talk about the fact that this is an actual evolutionary function. Partially because this is pretty new research, and also because it's kinda weird when you think about it.

We don't just tell stories because we want to . . . we *have* to. It's a biological human drive. In fact, humans are so wired to tell stories that we even do it in our sleep. This is why we dream.

The brain has a default mode. Everything essentially has a default mode, right? Some sort of resting state. A light switch turned off is in default mode. When you turn on the light, you activate it.

When the brain is activated, it's to concentrate on some kind of outside input. Someone talking to you, a problem to solve, someone to attend to, something that needs to be done that requires concentration. The rest of the time, the brain is in default mode. Awake and aware but generally resting.

Researchers have been able to map the brain in default mode . . . and here is where it gets really interesting. The brain in default mode is the storytelling brain!

So, our brain in resting state is when we story tell. You've totally caught yourself doing this. You're headed home. Nothing you need to do, you know this route so well, you aren't really engaged. Storytelling mode: activate. You're telling yourself a story about what you are going to eat later, or watch on TV, or chores you need to do. These conversations aren't bullet pointed reminder lists . . . you actually walk through a story of your plan.

A storytelling brain is an excellent thing most of the time.

- Stories are often rehearsals for life events, which makes them really useful if we are getting ready to field test a new skill.

- Stories allow us to hold larger chunks of information than we could otherwise. The PFC is designed to hold about seven pieces of information (plus or minus two). We try to juggle more than that, we start dropping things off the list. Stories, however, help us hold tons more information because they create pathways for remembering far more than we could otherwise.

- Stories are our primary mode of communication with others. According to Lewis Mehl-Madrona, MD, PhD—who incorporates Western medicine practices with the Lakota, Cherokee, and Cree ancestors and teachers—stories are how we relate to the world and share that information with others.

But clearly the storytelling brain can be a serious problem, too. We start telling ourselves (and believing) certain stories about ourselves and the world around us that aren't necessarily the whole truth. Like we walk into a room and a few people sitting in the corner burst out laughing. Our brain may decide they were laughing at us. And they don't like us. And they are laughing at us all the time. And we aren't safe even being around them. And the whole time, they were looking at llama videos on TikTok or whatever.

Our brains are wired to crave certainty. We want to see patterns in what happens so we can make better decisions about the world and how we are supposed to keep ourselves safe in it. But brains are stubborn, and they already have a story they've put together about what is real and true about the world.

You've seen that right? No matter what evidence to the contrary someone sees, they are determined to stay on course with their decision, no matter how dangerous or dumb. It's why elections can be so bizarre. Or people lose a fortune in a casino. The emotional brain makes a decision for us, and the thinking brain has to scramble to come up with a reason why.

Brains will rationalize *anything*.

YES, YOU CAN RETRAIN YOUR BRAIN

Since brains are adaptable, you can absolutely become friends again by retraining your brain. Don't believe me? Well, first of all you should. I'm a fancy doctor. But if you are one of those "Whatever, I want proof!" people, go to YouTube and search for "Lumiere Brothers Arrival of a Train." It's only a forty-five-second clip. I'll wait here.

So picture this: Paris. 1895. These brothers were photography pioneers who presented the first "moving picture" of a train pulling into a station at a public art exhibition. They were totes excited about their project ... but didn't get the expected response.

Instead, the moviegoers freaked out and all screamed in terror and hid under the seats. Like, every single one.

The brain's way of perceiving information was telling them all, "TRAIN ABOUT TO HIT YOU AND KILL YOU DEAD, GET OFF THE TRACKS!"

Because, yeah. Trains were dangerous, and moving images of trains did not exist until that point. Their brains perceived the train as a reality instead of a movie.

When you watched this, did your brain freak out? Duh, no. You know what a movie is. Your brain has been trained to understand a YouTube train versus a literal train.

And now your brain needs to learn real danger versus perceived danger. Remember that everybody's brain has issues with deciding what is a problem and what isn't, especially when it comes to survival. Like the toddler who calls all animals *doggies* until they learn that there are also *horsies* and *kitties* and *llamas* and *great white sharks*. The brain is going around yelling *doggie, doggie, doggie* all the time, even when it's wrong.

In this case, the amygdala just wants to scream DOGGIE!!! at the top of its lungs, and it doesn't trust that the PFC can tell the difference between a dog and anything else that may or may not be dangerous. We have to convince the PFC and the amygdala to hug it out and do their respective jobs, which means working together.

IT'S OFFICIAL. YOU ARE NOT CRAZY. A DOCTOR JUST SAID SO.

Yeah, that was a lot to read about the brain, but it was all important. Because it means that what we are doing, what we are thinking, and how we are feeling *make sense*.

Whether you find yourself all defensive and fight-y, freaking out, or completely shut off and shut down, that's your survival mode responding. The problem is when this happens during situations that aren't actually life-threatening emergencies. The amygdala has hijacked your ability to manage the situation in a rational way using the PFC.

It is not a *"Hey, let's investigate this situation, have a conversation about it, and then determine how we want to respond based on what will best benefit us in the long run"* kind of thinking. Your amygdala screamed, "DUCK

AND COVER!" and all rational responses went out the window.

Duck-and-cover thinking isn't always bad. It's the kind of thinking we need when we hear gunshots or tornado sirens. We *need* our brain to override our thought process if we accidentally touch a hot stove. If we didn't, that would mean that while our hand is burning, we are going through some long intellectual process of the experience while our amygdala and brainstem are in the background. This is not a YouTube video, this is life. We want a brain whose job is to keep us alive, right? Not just remember our locker combination from sixth grade and all the lyrics to Taylor Swift's "Shake It Off."

But in the process, it also protects us from everything it thinks *might* be danger, not just *actual* danger. Our ability to discriminate between *real* danger and *maybe* danger is an imperfect system. The brain is going to err on the side of caution, even if that means you shut down when you don't actually need to.

Say you are just trying to grab a sandwich somewhere, but you walk past flowers and your brain goes, "FLOWERS! ROY G BIV! ABORT MISSION!" And you are in a full-blown panic attack, running out of the store before you pass out. And you still don't have your sandwich.

You are all, "*Hey, Self, that was literally just flowers. Like roses or whatever. No one died, and now I'm hungry and didn't get my lunch.*" Or maybe you are not even sure why you lost it and are thinking, "*Damn, Self, what was that about?*"

That rational part? The *"just flowers, simmer down"* part? That requires **stimulus discrimination.** You know. *The ability to decide if something is actually a problem or not.*

Stimulus discrimination is a thinking thing, not an emotions thing. Which means it happens in the PFC, and once the brainstem gets into freak-out mode, it's really hard to get the PFC up and running again. But we can do it. And we are going to talk about how we retrain our brain to respond in ways that better suit life as it is now instead of life as it was in the past.

Our stimulus discrimination response is based on all of our past experiences and habits, and that response gets stronger when those experiences are traumatic. If a stimulus is attached to a strong memory, the body starts sending out all kinds of signals to prepare itself for response. Brains don't really have new thoughts so much as different versions of old thoughts.

This is why a military veteran may freak out at seeing garbage by the side of the road. If they were in Iraq, they were trained to look for bombs on the side of the road that were disguised to look like bags of trash.

Or if someone was abused, they may associate a certain smell with their abuser, like how their house smelled or the smell of the soap their abuser used.

The brain remembers that important stuff. It has been trained to do whatever it can to remain safe. It's creating stories about your current experience or possible future experiences based on its past information. It doesn't realize or doesn't trust that you actually are safe.

TAKE ACTION: TRIGGER IS NOT JUST ROY ROGERS' HORSE

We throw around the word trigger on the internetz like it's confetti or something. But a **trigger**, in this context, just means *the cause part of a cause-and-effect type situation going on.*

Sometimes we know straight up what our triggers are gonna be. For example, anxiety may be what you deal with the most. You may know that a first date, or speaking in front of a group, or a meeting with your teacher or parent is going to send your anxiety through the roof. But sometimes? No clue. Like all other mental health issues, we may have a genetic predisposition to certain responses, and/or it may be a product of the environment we grew up in or live in now. And that can make figuring out our specific triggers difficult.

Next time you start feeling yourself getting into eject mode, ask yourself these questions. And later, when you've cooled off, write the answers down:

• What specific emotion were you feeling? Those possible emotions again:

JOYFUL   EXCITED

Cheerful   satisfied

FRUSTRATED   cozy

angry   CALM

Sad   Despairing

Amused   SURPRISED

Confuzed   nervous

ANNOYED   Worried

- On a 0-100 scale, how would you rate that emotion? 100 being the worst it has even been in your life. So, like, 50 would be half that bad (and still really bad, right?)

- What did you notice in your body?

- What else was going on when it hit? Just write down everything that was going on, no matter how dumb or low-key you think it was. Because tracking patterns over time is how we figure out our triggers.

Another method is to keep a mood tracking diary (either an app or old school paper one). This feels like a lot of work but can really help with figuring out your triggers until you get the hang of doing it mentally throughout your day. On the next page is a simple format you can copy and use.

WEEKLY MOOD TRACKER

AM I IN A BAD MOOD OR... DO YOU SUCK?

	MOOD	SITUATION	MAGNITUDE (0-100)	SYMPTOMS
SUNDAY				
MONDAY				
TUESDAY				
WEDNESDAY				
THURSDAY				
FRIDAY				
SATURDAY				

CHAPTER TWO
HOW TRAUMA REWIRES THE BRAIN

OKAY, LADY, WHAT EXACTLY DO YOU MEAN BY TRAUMA?

A **trauma** is *an event that happens outside our understanding of how the world is supposed to work.* A **traumatic response** (also referred to as **traumatic stress**) *happens when our ability to cope with something that happened to us gets messed up, and it's affecting other areas of our life.*

There are lots of things that can operate as a trauma. To be honest, there are plenty of things that are deeply traumatic for many people that aren't listed in the manuals we are supposed to be using to diagnose people. It's one of the things that bugs me because it leads to people feeling ashamed that their trauma wasn't "traumatic enough" to warrant attention. And that sucks. Because fancy terms and definitions aside? A trauma is a "What was *that*?" situation.

A trauma can be an accident, an injury, a serious illness, a loss ... or any kind of life event that hurts you or breaks you in a long-lasting way.

But in the end? We all experience trauma differently and are impacted by too many things to list. Listing only the big "official" (diagnosable) categories dismisses other experiences that shouldn't be dismissed.

Recent studies show that about 75 percent of people living in the US will experience an event that exists on the "official" list. And while not all of them will develop PTSD, most people will spend a decent amount of time being pretty messed up, at least for a while. Suffering abuse as a child is a trauma we all recognize, for example. But dealing with horrific bullying isn't necessarily a recognized trauma ... even though many people have taken their own lives because they were bullied. So no list. But trauma doesn't operate by checking the right box in the right category. Instead? Please believe me when I say *your experiences and reactions are valid and real, and you are worthy of care and the opportunity to heal.*

We don't know why some things are worse than others for some people. I know it is a weird idea, but *everyone is different.* Everyone's lives, histories, and experiences are different, and our genetic predispositions are different, meaning that the way we react to trauma can actually be influenced by our genes.

And then, get this: We now even know that trauma can actually create genetic changes that can be passed down through generations! If you have a great-grandparent, grandparent, or parent with a serious trauma history, you are wired for a different response than someone who had family members without a lot of life drama. So not only do our genes influence our trauma reactions, our trauma reactions influence our genes.

On a physical level, traumatic response = amygdala hijack.

And there are different levels of intensity within that amygdala response. Sometimes we aren't in full-blown trauma mode, but we keep noticing some weird patterns and habits in our thinking and behavior. We don't act the same as we used to, or we realize that managing ourselves is taking away more energy than it should.

Short version? We all have our fragile places; we can't be completely tough about everything all the time, though what gets to us and what doesn't can end up being surprising.

HOW OUR BRAINS HANDLE TRAUMA

In a perfect world, bad things wouldn't happen. Heh, yeah. Good luck to all of us on that one. Second-best scenario is that when bad things happen, we are able to roll with it and come out unharmed. And, honestly, we do most of the time. About two-thirds of the time, when we experience a trauma, our brains don't go haywire. That means that *most of the time* we are eventually able to find a way to make sense of the trauma and recover from it without having enormous long-term consequences. This doesn't mean you didn't deal with something legit awful. It just means you were able to find your way through the experience without a long-term amygdala hijack.

Most of the time, it takes about three months to feel steady again after a trauma. That is, after about ninety days, our emotional sensors are no longer operating at hyper-warp-speed mode, and they return to normal.

Using the word *normal* isn't the best description, though. It's not *really* normal, no matter how well you recover. Traumas change us forever. So this so-called normal is more of a *new normal*. We find a way to live and cope with the situation that happened, the loss of what the world had been, and an acceptance of what it is now. We still experience feelings surrounding whatever happened—feelings that may never completely go away. But our amygdala isn't super haywire over the situation after a few months. Hijack mode, deactivated.

But approximately a third of the time, after a trauma, we don't recover to that new normal. We have a trauma response instead. And we may develop PTSD.

What is PTSD? The Oxford dictionary defines post-traumatic stress disorder as *"A condition of persistent mental and emotional stress occurring as a result of injury or severe psychological shock, typically involving disturbance of sleep and constant vivid recall of the experience, with dulled responses to others and to the outside world."*

Good definition. Fancy one. But the unfancy version? **PTSD** is *failure to recover from a traumatic event.* And PTSD is awful.

The National Center for PTSD (ptsd.va.gov) has collected research in this regard. What makes you more likely to experience PTSD? A lot of the indicators they found make a ton of sense:

- Being directly exposed as a victim or an in-person witness to a traumatic event

- Experiencing something that was very severe, or the person was hurt badly as a result of the incident

- Traumas that were long-lasting

- Believing you were in danger, or someone you loved was, and feeling helpless to protect them or yourself

- Having had a severe physical or emotional response during the traumatic situation

Our backgrounds can make us more susceptible to a trauma response, as well:

- Having had other traumas at a young age

- Having other mental health problems or having family members with mental health problems

- Having little support from family or friends, either by not having many individuals or being surrounded by individuals who don't understand your experience

- Having recently had stressful life changes or having recently lost a loved one

- Being female or in a minority cultural group (because you are statistically more likely to experience a trauma to begin with)

- Already using mind-altering substances like drugs or alcohol

- Being younger

- Having less education

- Coming from a cultural group or family system where you are less likely to talk about problems

The last item on that list is HUGE. Go read that again. When we talk about things, they get better.

But why? Why some people and not others? What's the brain science behind all of this?

Research shows that when we can't get to a new normal, it's because the brain's ability to process the experience is disrupted during the first thirty days after the trauma happened. **If ninety days is the basic timeframe for reestablishing balance, the first thirty days are the most fragile and necessary part of that process.** This is why PTSD cannot be diagnosed in the first month. We don't know yet if we're going to recover or not. **Those first thirty days are critical.**

We need time and space to recover, to process what happened, to find ways to make sense of the difference between how we want the world to work and our experience of how life actually unfolds. We need people around who get that and can support us. Our brains are hardwired to connect, and we get better in connection to other people. We'll dig into this in Chapter 3. Not having this time and these connections is a red flag that we are heading into trauma response territory. And not having this time, or these people, happens for a lot of really good reasons.

See, generally speaking, traumas are not stand-alone experiences. Trauma is a big mess of a lot of different things happening over an extended period of time. For example, people who have been abused well know that the abuse happens more than once. Trauma puts us in survival mode for that first thirty days. And if we're being continuously exposed to more trauma, we don't have any time and space to recover. The brain is actually being protective and shutting down your trauma processing when it says, "We are still trying to survive over here and can't really deal with the consequences right now!"

Sometimes it isn't a matter of continued trauma but the demands of our everyday lives that cause this shutdown. Sometimes we don't have the time and space to heal from our grief experience. Because we have to keep getting up in the morning and taking care of business. There is only so much work our overtaxed brain can handle. And sometimes our brain just has no way to make sense of the trauma. No matter how much time and space we give ourselves for healing, we can't find a place in our brain for the traumatic experience that gives it the meaning we need to move on. That's the storytelling brain again, stuck in telling the same story that just doesn't work.

Whatever the reason, the brain can shut down the healing process at a moment's notice, and our "new normal" is colored by trauma versus healing. This is called a **trauma-informed experience**. We start avoiding any reminders of our trauma because compartmentalizing is the only way we feel safe. And human beings are seriously adaptive. Avoiding can work really well for a really long time.

WHAT TRAUMA LOOKS LIKE ON AN ORDINARY DAY

How do you know you're dealing with trauma?

There are several ways that your brain tries to cope with trauma responses:

- *Arousal* – The amygdala is always wearing its crazy pants, and you find yourself freaked out when you shouldn't be or don't want to be. You may or may not know why. But your brain may process something it considers a threat that you aren't even aware of, and all of a sudden, you are falling apart in the middle of the store.

- *Avoidance* – You find yourself avoiding things that trigger arousal. Store was bad? I can order things online. I don't need to leave the house for groceries, right?

- *Intrusion* – Thoughts, images, memories related to the trauma experience start shoving their way up. The things that your brain was protecting you from don't actually go away. And they start bubbling to the surface without your consent or willingness. Intrusion happens when stuff shows up when least expected. And you can't manage everything that is bubbling up.

- **Negative Thoughts and Feelings** – With all this other stuff going on is it any wonder that you never just feel good? Or even just okay?

These experiences are how we diagnose full-blown PTSD. When they're present, it means that at some level you are reliving your trauma in your head at any given moment.

But not everyone having a trauma response has full-blown PTSD. A PTSD diagnosis is a checklist, in the end. Someone who is evaluating you for this diagnosis will be looking to see if you have a certain number of these symptoms. So some people meet *some* of the criteria for PTSD but not enough of them to receive that diagnosis.

But not meeting criteria for PTSD does not put you in the all-clear or make you magically feel any better, right? You are clearly not okay now, and there is a pretty good chance that it is gonna get worse if you're not working on getting better.

The Department of Veterans Affairs (the VA) figured this out when studying first responders after the Twin Towers in New York and the Pentagon in Washington, DC, were attacked on 9/11. Of the people who had some symptoms of a trauma response but not full-blown PTSD after the attack, 20 percent showed a symptom increase two years later that qualified them for a PTSD diagnosis. *Go figure* that if you keep reliving your trauma, those connections keep reinforcing in your brain, getting worse and worse each time.

Thoughts, feelings, and behaviors that are driven by our trauma response can be really difficult things to understand. Not just for the people around us but even for ourselves. Have you ever had a moment like that? When you were thinking, "What is wrong with me? Why am I acting like this?" We feel clueless, and the people who love us feel helpless.

Let's give our brains a break here, though, because it's the brain out there trying to make sense of the world when the world itself isn't making sense. So it goes all over-reactive in how it demands you respond to certain events. It reminds you of your stories. And those certain memories trigger negative emotions. And the brain reacts in a protective way without you even realizing what's going on.

Okay then. What kinds of symptoms do we need to watch out for? Good question, smart cookie! The list is a pretty long one.

Reliving the Trauma Symptoms:

- Feeling like you are reliving the trauma even though it's behind you, and you are physically safe

- Dreaming you are back in the traumatic event (or maybe a similar event where you feel super out of control)

- Having a huge emotional response when something or someone reminds you about the trauma. Like freaking out, even though you are currently safe. And/or lots of physical symptoms (sweating, heart racing, sweating, fainting, breathing problems, headaches, etc.)

Avoiding the Memories of the Trauma Symptoms:

- Doing things to distract yourself from thoughts or feelings about the trauma and/ or avoiding talking about it when it comes up

- Avoiding things associated with the trauma like people, places, and activities. And a lot of times these areas of avoidance get bigger and bigger. Like avoiding a certain street that an accident happened on, then the whole neighborhood, then driving in a car at all

- Needing to feel in control in all circumstances, like sitting in spots that feel safest in public places, not wanting people in your space, avoiding crowds. (Some people do this because of safety training—being in a military family, living in a sketchy neighborhood—so it's a deliberate response and not a sign of PTSD.)

- Having a hard time remembering/having blocked out important details of the trauma

- Feeling totally numb or detached from everything or just about everything

- Not interested in regular activities and fun stuff—stuff you used to like and just don't anymore

- Not being connected to your feelings and moods in general. Feeling just . . . blank

- Not seeing a future for yourself, like just more of the same versus things getting better

Other Medical or Emotional Symptoms:

- Stomach upset, trouble eating, only craving foods that are sugary (therefore more comforting to a stressed out body)

- Trouble falling asleep or staying asleep. Or sleeping a lot but not well. Either way, feeling exhausted all the time

- Not having enough energy to take care of yourself in important ways (exercising, eating healthy foods, getting regular health care, safer sex with chosen partners)

- Soothing symptoms away with substances (e.g., drugs, alcohol, nicotine use, food) or behaviors (e.g., gambling, shopping, or dumb endorphin-producing games like playing chicken with trains)

- Getting sick more frequently or noticing that chronic physical health issues are getting worse

- Anxiety, depression, guilt, edginess, irritability, and/or anger. (A HUGE number of mental health diagnoses are really just a trauma response that is not being properly treated, sadly.)

Is it any wonder that we get all confused about what is a trauma response versus some other diagnosis? So the easy diagnosis is PTSD. But trauma responses, like I mentioned above, can wear a Halloween mask of other stuff. Depression and anxiety are two big ones. Sometimes trauma responses can even hide themselves as bipolar disorder and schizophrenia. I have worked with more than one person that had a label of a thought disorder like schizophrenia, but when we started discussing the content of their "voices" we realized they were trauma flashbacks. Other ways that trauma responses disguise themselves can be ADHD, anger and irritability, attachment and relationship issues, and a twisted sense of right and wrong.

There is nothing wrong with any of these other diagnoses in and of themselves. Diagnoses can be necessary to get insurance to pay for services. They also serve as a tool among clinicians as a shorthand that is only meant to say, "These symptoms are present." And these diagnoses can absolutely exist on their own, without a trauma trigger. When trauma *is* the root cause, trauma-related diagnoses are actually more successfully treated than many other mental health issues—*if we understand what the symptoms are a response to and handle them in that context.*

Our brain doesn't have to be enemy territory forever. Brain befriending is a completely possible thing.

TAKE ACTION: NAME IT

Give your negative reactions an actual persona to inhabit. Name them after a crappy teacher or an evil RPG character. Create a whole character.

Emotions feel so huge that transforming them into an actual, defined entity that you can battle *really helps.* Then you can have convos with *Donald Trump's Epic Hair Swirl* (or whomever your entity is) whenever it comes calling.

Now you can focus on that entity the way you would on an actual person threatening you in a real-world situation. You can negotiate, you can yell back, you can lock it in a box. It's now at a manageable size of your choosing, with the appropriate amount of ridiculousness that you can laugh at while you show it who's in charge.

CHAPTER 3:
BEFRIEND YOUR BRAIN

If we called the first two chapters of this book "This Is Your Brain," the rest of this book would be called "This Is Your Brain on Therapy."

Trauma is like a wound that has crusted over the top but hasn't fully healed. It looks closed over, but the infection is still burrowed in under the skin even when we don't realize it is there or when we find ways to ignore it. But what happens if we don't clean out that wound? It festers.

We have to clean it out for it to heal. We create new ways to feel safe that don't cause us more harm in the long run. We process our experiences with people who are safe and trustworthy and care about us. We retrain our brains to *think* rather than *react*. Those wounds? *We treat them.*

But what about the scar it leaves behind? Well, scars are reminders that we healed.

THE FANCY SCIENCE OF BEFRIENDING

Because our emotions are tied so closely in the brain to our memory, it makes sense that memories of past events alongside current experiences can cause a really strong response.

But our brains aren't actually wired to hold onto certain emotions for long periods of time. Emotions are designed as part of our information feedback circuit.

WE LIKE THAT! MORE OF THAT!

or

THAT SUCKS! MAKE IT STOP!

Our emotions influence our thoughts and behaviors. They are meant to be signals to the rest of the brain. Once they have done their jobs, they are then meant to dissipate.

Do you know how long an emotion is actually meant to last? Ninety seconds.

Seriously, just one and a half minutes for an emotion to run its course.

You may not believe me, right now, I know. Because if that were really the case, why do our emotions last hours, days, or years? Ninety seconds? Not so much.

Emotions last longer than ninety seconds because we continue to fuel them with our thoughts. We do this by telling ourselves the same stories about the triggering situation over and over.

We also continue to fuel them with our behaviors. My favorite definition of crazy is *doing the same thing over and over and expecting different results.* So when we are reactive instead of proactive, we keep reinforcing the pattern. It's no longer an emotional response, it's a whole *mood.*

Say you were in a terrible car accident while driving down First Street. It makes total sense that being in a car driving down First Street after the accident would send your brain into a panic. So you avoid First Street. Eventually avoiding First Street is such a habit that anything that involves being near First Street doesn't happen. You don't *want* to have a meltdown over the thought of driving down First Street. You want your life back! But as long as you continue to avoid First Street, you are deepening the groove of that behavior and the feelings of panic that you associate with remembering the accident.

Thinking about the accident becomes something you can't control. **Rumination** is *a form of unwelcome, obsessive attention to our own thought patterns.*

It's a stuck point. An error in the coding. We ruminate about the accident to the point of thinking we are losing our minds because it feels like the rumination has taken control.

Basically, we continue to feed that particular emotional response (anxiety, fear) and those particular thoughts (accidents happen on First Street) by continuing with the same adaptive strategies we originally used to keep ourselves safe (don't drive down First Street, bad things happen there!). So we keep the feedback circuit going in a nonstop loop.

Okay, yeah, maybe. But what about all those non-rumination memories? The feelings we will go to the end of the earth to avoid? Instead, maybe you refuse to give *any* attention at all to the idea of driving down First Street. Ruminate? Not the problem. That's our brain wiring again. Avoiding a certain emotion makes you hold on to it just as much as ruminating over it does. Remember the infection analogy? It's just festering in there.

When we hit upon a situation where control is taken away from us, even the memory of that event is seriously awful. It's a reminder that we have far less control over the world than our brain wants to have. Both rumination and avoidance are ways our brain reacts in an attempt to get control back. If I fixate on it, I can figure out a way to keep it from happening again. If I avoid it, I can erase it from existence in the past, present, and future. It feels way safer than remembering something, recognizing it for the event that it was, and then letting it go.

To get to a place where we just feel what we feel? To sit with it for that ninety seconds? To remember that it's just information from our body, part of our feedback circuit? That it doesn't define us or change anything about the essence of who we are? That it may not even be accurate information about the situation? Really hard.

Remember all that fancy brain stuff from the first chapter? Because our brains are hardwired to keep us alive, the instinctual part of our brain takes over when we feel threatened. But unlike the other species we share this planet with, when the threat is over, we aren't good at discharging that threat feeling, getting all those hormones and neurotransmitters out of our system, and going back to our everyday lives.

And the PFC (remember the prefrontal cortex?) cannot *control* our instinctual responses; it can offer different information, advice, and possibilities for responding. It can negotiate, but it is not in charge in times of high stress. You are not crazy for wondering if your thinking brain has been hijacked by your animal brain. You feel that way *because it has*.

And quite frankly, your animal brain is irritated at all your epic ingratitude at how hard it is working to keep you alive.

It's not a sign of weakness that it keeps happening. It's a hard-wired survival instinct. You can't forcibly take control back through sheer willpower. Animal brain will win every time.

Healing trauma means working through what happened to us, rather than trying to overpower it.

DEALING WITH TRAUMA RIGHT AFTER IT HAPPENS

Okay, remember when I was yammering about all that first thirty / ninety days stuff? That this is a really critical time for trauma recovery? Yeah. Because if we are given the time and space to process a huge, horrible thing that happened to us? That makes all the difference in the world.

Talking about what happened is a good first step for most people, but just going through the facts isn't enough. Focusing on "just the facts" rather than processing emotional memories has the potential to separate us even further from the emotional content of our experience.

When any event happens, it transforms in that instant from an occurrence to a memory. If we are given the space and support, we are empowered to process that memory on the emotional level it was stored at. *"Just the facts"* is only meant to be the beginning of the healing process because it is not nearly as helpful as *"all the feels."*

So if someone has handed you this book after a very recent trauma event? They are saying they are there and want to help. Or maybe you picked it up yourself because the little voice in the back of your head said you should. Either way? This is the time to take care of yourself. You need the space to heal.

I haven't really found a huge difference between the things that help you heal when a trauma is fresh versus what to do when it is older. But I have found that healing is way easier when we dig into it right away and don't give our brains the opportunity to start mapping out signals that mess us up. I also found that if you're able to do the work now, you are far less likely to struggle with chronic mental illness as a result of your trauma, or at least it will be less severe/ more manageable.

And I also know you are worth the time it takes to focus on yourself and your healing. No matter how silly it feels, or how busy you are, or how much everyone around you is dismissive or uncomfortable with the process.

You deserve every opportunity to heal.

DEALING WITH THINGS WAY LATER

Then there are those of us who didn't get a chance to really unpack our trauma during that ninety-day re-stabilization window. This just means there are more months or years to untangle. This is not a hopeless situation at all. Because if this is you? You are a SURVIVOR. Your brain figured out ways to keep you going when everything around you was crazy. And it worked.

The problem is, it isn't working well anymore. Instead of being a solution, it's become a problem. So your brain has to be put back on its leash and retrained.

You need to teach your brain to use your PFC to distinguish between real threats and perceived threats again. When the feedback system works the way it's intended to, the amygdala doesn't go nuts and send every message to the brainstem to activate freak-out mode.

A lot of the work I do in my private practice is guiding people through processing their stories while helping them stay grounded in the present. This helps us remember that we are in control of our experience at this point in our lives, even if we weren't in the past. It is amazing to realize you can feel something and not have it overwhelm you. That right there? That is what *taking your power back* really means.

Many people do this work in therapy, but not everyone. Even if you are working with a therapist, a good therapist is going to operate as your sideline coach, giving suggestions and feedback from the outside perspective. If you are working through any of these issues, you are the one doing the hard part, whether your supports are friends, family, or helping professionals, or just your own determination to get better.

Whether you have help or are going it on your own, I've found that knowing why these techniques work make them work that much faster. Knowing how the brain is wired to work helps us feel less frustrated, stupid, and guilty. Because one of the biggest barriers to getting better? Shame. Shame from ourselves and shame from others that we aren't already better. Or that we had an issue to begin with.

And no one deserves that.

Remember what I said about you being a survivor? If you have crawled through all these months or years of muck, fighting with a haywire brain, YOU DESERVE TO FEEL BETTER. You deserve your life back. You are not unfixably broken.

Let's do this thing.

OKAY, SO IT'S NOT REALLY A TRAUMA. BUT I STILL HAVE A MESSED-UP BRAIN. WHAT'S UP WITH THAT?

So you picked up this book because you figured you have some work to do. But the trauma stuff doesn't really ring a bell for you. That's not your thing. But you don't like some of the stuff going on in your head and want to do something about it.

Maybe you have a habit of reacting that's less intense than a trauma response but works essentially the same way. Even if your amygdala isn't in terrorist hijack mode, your memories and emotions are still wired together, right? Your amygdala has its groove going in a bad habit, making life harder for you in dumb ways.

What is a **habit**? *A settled or regular tendency or practice, especially one that is hard to give up.* You did something, and it worked. You continued to do it, and it continued to work. At some point maybe it stopped working as well, if at all, but your brain is still grooving along with the story that it works because it hasn't figured out a better option. So it's still going to trigger an amygdala response, tying memory to emotion. It may not be a hugely overactive trauma-informed response, but it is there nonetheless.

This is why addictions are so hard to treat. Learning to stop doing something is really hard once we have wired a particular response. Hence the "Addictions" chapter of this book. Even if you are all, *"Yeah, not messing with drugs or alcohol, doesn't apply,"* consider reading it anyway. Pretty much great info for everybody.

And yes, behaviors and thinking patterns can *totally* feel addictive and out-of-control even if they aren't true addictions.

For example, maybe you live in a house where no one talks about their feelings. It isn't encouraged and everyone else becomes uncomfortable if you try. You probably learned pretty quickly that talking about your feelings is clearly against the rules. You aren't abused or traumatized. But, at the dinner table, if you say, *"My best friend and I had a fight today, and I'm really sad and angry,"* your parent might say, *"That happens sometimes, dear, please pass the potatoes."*

So if you try talking about your feelings and are continuously shut down, you will probably wire a connection in your brain that having these discussions makes other people uncomfortable. This can make you feel anxious, or guilty, or frustrated on top of the feelings you were already working hard to express.

The good news is that the info in Chapter 4 will work for you, too. And it will work faster because the story doesn't have the far deeper groove that a trauma creates. Your work will be more about recognizing patterns than deeper rewiring.

I LOVE SOMEONE WITH A SERIOUS TRAUMA HISTORY

This is seriously tough, isn't it? You have someone that you care about so much who is really struggling with their trauma recovery. You want to help. And feeling unable to do so is the worst feeling in the world. You're at risk of serious burnout and even having a trauma reaction by being so close to someone else's trauma. Because, yeah, watching someone live out their trauma can be a traumatic experience in and of itself.

Two things to remember, here:

- This is not your battle.

- . . . but people do get better in supportive relationships.

This is not your battle. You don't get to plan their healing for them. You don't get to determine what makes something better, what makes something worse. No matter how well you know someone, you don't know their inner processes. *They* may not even know their inner processes. If you know someone well, you may know a lot. But you're not the one living their life.

Telling someone what they should be doing, feeling, or thinking won't help. Even if you are right. Even if they do what you say . . . you have just taken away their power to do the work they need to do to take charge of their life. There are limits to how much better they can really be if they are continually rescued by you.

. . . but people do get better in supportive relationships. The best thing to do is to ask your loved one how to best support them when they are struggling. This is the type of action plan you can create with a therapist (if either or both of you are seeing one) or ask them in a private conversation.

Ask them. Ask if they want help grounding when they are triggered, if they need time alone, anything else. Ask what you can do and do those things, if they are healthy things to provide.

It may be helpful for them to have a formal safety plan for themselves (there is a sample safety plan at the end of this book) including what your specific role will be. This will help give boundaries to your role and keep you from setting up scenarios where you rescue or enable dangerous and/or self-sabotaging behavior.[2]

You may need to set hard limits. You may need to protect yourself. This isn't just for your well-being but will help you model the importance of doing so to your loved one.

2 This is also a great resource to use for yourself! Or everyone. We're all one really bad event from being in a crisis; having strategies in place to get us through whatever comes our way is always a good idea.

Love the entirety of them. Remind them that their trauma doesn't define them. Allow them consequences of their behavior and celebrate the successes of newer, healthier ways of being. Be the relationship that helps the healing journey.

TAKE ACTION: RIDE THE WAVE

Emotions last ninety seconds. And because you are NOT AT ALL the type of person who reads the text boxes before the actual main text (unlike me), you know that means that emotions are meant to be a signal in the brain that something needs your attention. They are meant to only last long enough to actually get your attention, and they dissipate after you decide on your course of action.

The problem is we tend to do one of two things instead of paying attention. We either get stuck thinking about it constantly or get stuck trying to avoid it constantly. Both make things worse.

Try setting aside five minutes to sit with the emotion you're feeling instead of fighting back. All this means is being mindful of your present emotional experience. You can freewrite as you are processing.

You can practice breathing. You can do anything other than avoid or distract from the feeling. The point is to retrain yourself that it won't last forever. You may feel overwhelmed for a few minutes, but this is not a permanent state of being.

If you attend to what you are feeling, you get over it way more quickly than if you avoid it. I've noticed I'm bored with myself about three minutes into committing to sitting with my feelings for five. I'm ready to go make a cup of coffee, read a book, find the cookies I hid from myself, or do *anything other than getting stuck in a loop for hours on end.*

TAKE ACTION: PUT IT ON ICE

A lot of therapists used to encourage clients to wear a rubber band and snap it on their wrist if they felt an urge to self-harm, or were having spinning thoughts, or were considering an impulsive behavior. But, um, snap a rubber band on yourself enough times, and you will tear up your skin. So we're not doing that anymore.

But the point of the rubber band was legit. We were trying to help people disrupt the current focus of the brain by encouraging it to attend to another pain point. Ice works much better without causing lasting damage. Seriously, try it. Grab an ice cube and squeeze. Your brain is gonna be all, "OW! What are you doing that for?" and it disrupts the signal. If you have an impulse to self-injure to manage anxiety, for instance, you can actually place the ice on the part of the body you typically hurt instead of doing the other harmful behavior.

The cool thing, too, is carrying ice with you isn't obvious. You can bop around in your day and grab an ice cube out of your cup without people going, "What the hell is that about?" I have worked in group programs where everyone carried water, so handing someone a cup full of ice to use if they got triggered didn't make them feel singled out to their peers.

CHAPTER 4
GETTING BETTER: RETRAIN YOUR BRAIN

A FRAMEWORK FOR GETTING BETTER

So this is the general "how" section of the book. Of course, not everyone has the same responses to situations. If they did, fixing things would be easy, and I wouldn't have a job. So topics related to some of the specific things that happen to people will come up in later chapters. You know . . . depression, anxiety, anger, addiction, grief responses, and stress. All parts of the human condition at some point in every life.

Life does what it does, and half the time we are just trying to keep up. So what other people call stages, I call a framework. It's good to have an idea of where you are in the process at any particular moment. So you can focus on what will work best *at that moment*. And if later on today (or next week, or next year) you are five steps forward or two steps back? That's where we go in. No biggie.

One of the best frameworks for understanding how the brain heals from trauma comes from Judith

Herman's book *Trauma and Recovery*. Her grown-person labels (and my less traditional ones) are listed below:

Safety and Stabilization
That's over, right? I can sit down for a second without something else awful happening? Would that be possible, Universe?

Remembrance and Mourning
What was that? What happened? Life isn't supposed to go down like that! That was AWFUL.

Reconnection
Okay. So, maybe, just maybe, the whole world isn't completely awful, and I can still generally be okay again. Not to say that wasn't bad. But not everything or everyone is bad.

Safety and Stabilization: If trauma means that our sense of safety in the world has been violated, regaining that sense of safety feels almost impossible. That event became a seriously strong memory that continuously triggers our *fight, flight, or freeze* response. Safety and stabilization is the process of understanding what is going on with your brain and taking back control over your body when this happens. It's the brain reboot when things get triggered for you. Herman's book focuses on this stage, and so does mine. Because it's the hardest part to get going . . . and nothing else happens without it.

Remembrance and Mourning: This is the part we call a *trauma narrative*. It's not just "This is what happened to me," like you're writing a book report of a Stephen King novel, but a way of working through the trauma as you remember it along with the thoughts and feelings that are bundled up with the event memories. It's the space to be allowed to process your story when you have the skills to do so without being triggered. It's about owning your story and not letting your story own you. If we think of trauma as emotions trapped in the body, this is how we get them to leave. This can be done in all kinds of safe ways: with a therapist, with an awesome loved one, in a support group, or even by yourself in a journal when outside support isn't available.

Reconnection: This is a fancy way of saying "taking your life back." It means finding a way to fit trauma into its rightful place within the entirety of your life, rather than it taking over and controlling every aspect of your life. It's about finding meaning in your experience. This can be so hard to wrap your head around, I know. This doesn't mean that the situation wasn't horrible, but it does mean that you can use it to make yourself stronger, to support others, to not let it own you. It means having positive relationships that are defined by *everything* you are instead of just your trauma. It can also be about reconnecting to your spirituality, if that has been an important part of your identity. It means knowing that no matter what else happens . . . you have YOU in your corner. A survivor anyone would be lucky to have on their side.

Okay, I admit it's easier to explain than to do, but let's talk about how to get started.

FIRST THINGS FIRST: SAFETY AND STABILIZATION

The following section is full of activities that engage the prefrontal cortex and override the brainstem takeover that puts you into *fight, flight, or freeze* response. Teaching the PFC to focus on something else disrupts the whole hostile takeover response.

Bruce Lipton, in his book *The Biology of Belief*, compares trying to stop an amygdala hijack to screaming at a tape player because you don't like the song that's on. Once the play button has been pushed, mechanics take over and logic doesn't enter the equation. A more modern analogy? My phone connects to my car as soon as I start it and enjoys blasting The Linda Lindas' cover of "Rebel Girl" literally every time. Not any other music I've downloaded, not any podcast I've downloaded. Only "Rebel Girl" will do. And yelling at my car, or my phone, or my bluetooth connection, or the music itself doesn't do anything to make it stop playing.

You CANNOT have a logical conversation directly with the amygdala. Anything you want to do has to be a negotiation with the amygdala by the PFC because the amygdala is in protection mode (or terrorist mode, depending on your patience at the moment) and is the one in charge. This is where we restabilize ourselves and reestablish our sense of safety. By getting our PFC to sneak in and pause the song, we can negotiate with the amygdala to chill out. Yes, you can actually do something else and think of something else. But you do have to train yourself how to.

This trauma response didn't creep up on you overnight, right? You didn't go to bed one night feeling all fine and dandy and wake up the next morning all kinds of hot mess. Your brain created its response network based on the information it was receiving over time, so learning to be healthy is also going to take time.

Some days are going to be better than others. You may do awesomely well then get hit like a ton of bricks with all kinds of what-just-happened??!!??

Those days are awful, aren't they?

None of that makes you a failure; it means you are still growing. I tell my clients, "It really is going to be okay in the end. If it's not okay yet, that means we aren't at the end."

And bits of okay now and then give us the breathing room and resting space to store energy for our next battle against that anxiety-trying-to-eat-our-face-off thingy. That's not the technical term, but it should be.

Practicing good coping skills and techniques while you are *not* in freak-out mode will make it easier to figure out which ones work best for you and then to access them when you *are* in freak-out mode. Having people around you who feel safe to you and can help prompt you to use your positive coping skills can be invaluable. Because as you well know, taking back control of your brain when it's been hijacked is really difficult.

There is an expression: *Amateurs practice until they get it right, experts practice until they can't get it wrong.* Proving you can do something once is easy. Getting so good at it that it becomes your second nature is way harder. But that's what rewires a trauma reaction. Do it so often it just becomes *what you do.* And when you are triggered, you'll use those coping skills.

Of course, it probably seems that panic comes on at the worst possible time, when you are in the middle of a crowded store with no one you know with you, for example. So having a set of simple coping skills as well as the more complicated ones is priceless. It might be a literal talisman (a stone you carry), a mantra you repeat, or the coping cards from the text box below. Yes, they seem cheesy. But they work so well, I gotta throw the idea out there.

TAKE ACTION: CREATE COPING CARDS

The problem with all the coping mechanisms that follow is that chances are you can't remember them in the heat of the moment, at least not at first. So when you find a mantra, a grounding exercise, a fact about anxiety, or another statement or image or action that helps you, put it on an index card. Hole punch your cards, put them on a snap-shut key ring, and you have a set of coping cards you can flip through when panic hits.

It sounds epically nerdy, I know. But I have had so many clients end up loving their cards and using them all the time. They're a way to remind the PFC to be in charge of the control stick and ground itself in reality. It's cheese with extra cheese sauce, but that's what works when we are actively rewiring the brain.

Grounding Techniques

I get asked a lot to teach *just one skill* to people. New counselors, new foster parents, and first responders who aren't counselors but end up helping people manage a mental health crisis all ask, *"What's the one universal thing that anyone can do to help someone having a rough time?"* The best answer I have is to help people ground themselves back in their bodies and in the present moment.

When triggered, the brain is reliving a past event instead of responding to the present moment. Grounding activities help you get back into your body and the present moment rather than reliving your memories. Grounding is one of the best ways to manage emotional pain because it reminds you that the pain itself is based in memory and doesn't have the power to hurt you in this moment.

Some people don't want to unpack their story and process their trauma. And that's okay. But everyone wants a way to manage what comes up when they are experiencing a trauma reaction. Grounding helps a lot. Seriously. It's the best way of saying, "*Hey, amygdala? Slow your roll.*"

Mental Grounding

Mental grounding techniques are intended to keep you in the present moment by focusing on your current situation and surroundings. You are gonna use mantras or make lists. And yes, you can say these out loud. To yourself, to someone else. If you're on the city bus and don't want to draw attention, you can go through your list mentally or mutter under your breath. Whatever works. (If you put in headphones, people will think you are singing to yourself, which weirds them out far less than talking to yourself.)

- You might describe all the colors in the room or an object you are holding.

- Repeat a safe phrase to yourself over and over. Like, "I know I'm safe right now."

- Some people like to play a kind of categories game, where they name all their favorite movies, or books, or something that requires a different kind of concentration.

- Some people will go over their schedule, either in their mind or out loud, or the steps needed to complete an activity.

All of these mental grounding activities are a way to remind your brain where you are in the moment and that you have more control than you realize over what is going on inside you when your panic button has been tripped.

Physical Grounding

As young children, we are in our bodies and in our experiences all the time. It isn't until we get older that we realize our bodies can be in one place while our mind goes somewhere else. This is great when your body is in math class and your brain is on the playground. But it becomes more problematic as we get older. Have you ever found yourself arriving at home without remembering anything about the trip it took to get there? Physical grounding techniques are ways of reminding us that we are in our bodies and that we have ownership of that experience.

- Simply notice your breathing, in and out. When you catch yourself wandering, remind yourself to focus back on the breath.

- You may try walking and noticing each step you take. If you find that you walk and still ruminate, try carrying a teaspoon of water while you walk, and focus on trying not to spill drops of it.

- Touch objects around you.

- Sometimes specific sensory objects are especially soothing. These are usually suggested for people who respond differently neurologically (you know, people with autism spectrum-type wiring), but they can help everyone. Things like a cotton ball with lavender oil on it kept in an airtight container that can be opened and sniffed to trigger a calming response. Something to chew on (gum, beef jerky). Play-Doh that can be squished, glitter bottles that can be shaken, a talisman in your pocket like a polished stone or something of spiritual significance. A ring that you can spin on your finger.

- Jump up and down.

- Make sure your feet are touching the floor. Try taking off your shoes and feeling the ground beneath you.

- Eat something slowly and be mindful of all the flavors and textures. Grapes or raisins work well for this. Interestingly? People who don't even like raisins (and I raise my hand here) are not bothered by them when using them for this exercise.

- If you feel safe to be touched, have someone you trust put their hands on your shoulders and remind you gently to remain in your body.

- If touch isn't going to make things worse, give someone a hug. Cuddle with your boo. Hold your little sibling's hand. Touching and being touched releases oxytocin. Touch is also good for the heart and the immune system. So get on that.

Soothing Grounding

Soothing grounding is essentially self-compassion and self-care in a difficult situation.

- Think of things that make you feel better. Visualize things you enjoy, such as the beach or a sunset. A sunset on the beach? I'm down with that.

- Remember a safe place and picture yourself surrounded by that safety.

- Plan an activity or treat you can look forward to in the near future, like a cupcake from your favorite bakery, a hot bath, a movie you've seen a hundred times and still adore, a baseball game and a bowl of popcorn, or a hike in your favorite park.

- Carry pictures of people and places you care about, and focus on these images.

You can play with all of these different forms of grounding and develop ones that work best for you when you are feeling most distressed. But above all else? You totally got this. Your brain has done its job keeping you safe, and now you are ready to take the reins back and move forward in your life. And that's excellent, isn't it?

Mindfulness Meditation

Okay, first of all let's start by getting all definition-y. We tend to use mindfulness and meditation as interchangeable terms. Or in a non-interchangeable-but-still-confusing way. They aren't really meant to be interchangeable, and they aren't really meant to be confusing either.

Meditation is when you intentionally set aside time to do something that's good for you. There are all kinds of meditations (prayer, exercise, art, etc.).

Mindfulness is both a general awareness of the world (noticing your existence and the existence of everything else around you) *and* can be a formal meditation practice. It's two things, not one.

So you can meditate without being particularly mindful, and you can be mindful without meditating. But meditation and mindfulness overlap when we do **mindfulness meditation**, which means that we are *setting aside time for intentional focus on our awareness of the world* ... which includes the workings of our own mind.

There are people who are way smarter than me about this. But here's the basic guideline to get you started:

Sit upright. If you can do this without back support, like on the floor on a cushion then good on you. If you need a straight back chair, do that. If you can't sit at all, that's okay, too. Get yourself in whatever position is most comfortable. The reason sitting is better than laying down is that the point is to fall awake, not fall asleep. But the point is also to not be in screaming pain, so don't stress it.

Soft-focus your eyes so they aren't closed, but they are seeing without actually seeing. You know what I mean. Be visually spaced out because what you are really going to be paying attention to is inside you.

And now you are going to breathe in and out. And focus on your breath. If you have never done this before, it's going to be weird and hard. But for *the record, if you have done this a zillion times chances are still good that it will be weird and hard.*

If you catch yourself being distracted, just label it "thinking" and go back to focusing on your breath. Thinking isn't a failure in the least. It's gonna happen. And noticing it and bringing the mind back to the present moment is the point. So it's a total win.

A lot of people feel awful during meditation, thinking they suck at it because they are continuously distracted by chatting thoughts. That's okay. Your brain is desperately seeking to storytell. All kinds of distracting stuff will come up. You are going to think about what you want to eat for dinner. Or a conversation you had at school. Or whether or not you should buy new sneakers or go to a movie this weekend.

The default network of the brain is storytelling mode, remember? And you aren't distracted by external events, so the default mode has all kinds of stories to tell you. But here is the thing about mindfulness meditation . . . research shows that it disrupts the storytelling process of the default network. We used to think the only way to do that was a distraction by outside events and stimulus.

I'm not even going to pretend that this is easy to do when you are spun up. But it's important to at least try. Because part of a panic attack is the stories our brain starts telling us about the attack itself. And it's generally not a pretty story. The chemicals released during an anxiety or panic attack are designed to get your breathing ramped up and your heart racing. So your brain is insisting that you are going to have a heart attack or stop breathing. That's not actually going to happen. When you catch that thinking, remind yourself that it's a biochemical response but not reality.

Keep breathing. The continued, conscious effort to breathe and untense will slow your heart rate back down and help you get more oxygen flowing. It's a literal chemical counterbalance. Meditation releases every chemical that counteracts a brain hijack: dopamine, serotonin, oxytocin, and endorphins. And it's free! Thousands of years of Buddhist practice has something going for it, yeah?

Treat your bodily reactions like any other random thought. Itching is common. If you catch yourself itching, label it *thinking* three times before succumbing to the urge to scratch. You may be surprised at how often your brain creates things for you to focus on. When I first started meditating, my nose would start to run. My meditation instructor got wise to my epically awesome self-distraction skill and started keeping tissues by her cushion for me. I wasn't allowed to get up. I used a tissue and went back to my breathing. Of course, if you have real pain, don't ever ignore that. Rearrange yourself for comfort, and don't be a hero.

If you have someone helping you through this, they can prompt your mindfulness by saying something like, "Hey, what are you noticing going through your head right now?" or progressive relaxation by saying, "Okay, let's start with your hands. They're really clenched up, can you spread out your fingers instead of balling your hands up?" Sometimes meditation feels more doable if you have someone meditating with you—it helps you feel supported and kept on track.

Prayer

So we just defined mindfulness meditation, right? Meditation is no more than **listening to.** Meditation is the process of quieting ourselves down enough to hear what's going on inside us. Our minds are brilliant at creating endless amounts of chatter that we often talk back to without listening first. Meditation is the willingness to hear yourself before you speak.

What does prayer have to do with it? You may be rolling your eyes up in your head at me over this one, I know. *Prayer? I don't do religion.* But what we have, as a culture, agreed to call prayer is just **talking to.** Speaking to ourselves or something bigger than ourselves about our wants, needs, desires, and intentions. Remember the storytelling brain? Prayer is a natural mechanism of the storytelling brain. Talking through our situation in this manner can be far more powerful than talking to a friend, family member, or therapist. It's a grounding experience that helps us be more aware of our thoughts, feelings, and behaviors. This is what is going on. This is what I want. This is the help that I need.

Music

Because who doesn't like music? Only the same people who hate the smell of home baked bread and don't understand how adorable fluffy baby sloths are.

Do you know how much of our day we spend listening to music? Like four hours. Music is primal.

Scientists recently figured out ways to prove that we have specific neurons in the brain that pay attention only to music, ignoring all other audial noises. Brains have music rooms! And, just maybe, music existed before speech did. And that's why speech developed at all . . . to go with our music. And look at how much of our early architecture was designed around our need for music. Across cultures, places of worship were designed around our need to create music in communion. Music is both primal and communal.

We all use music in different ways. Some people want music that is soothing when they are distressed. Others want to hear things that are loud and thrashy and match what is going on inside. Still others want things that are upbeat and danceable.

I grew up listening to old blues albums on vinyl while the other, less weird kids were watching *Sesame Street*. So guess what is most soothing for me? Old blues albums on vinyl. Or when I need a pick-me-up, I like to pull up the music I work out to. It has a cadence that I connect to physical movement. I may use it to dance to while cleaning the house or even while driving to prepare myself for the event I'm driving to.

What works for you?

Having music that helps your brain connect to either a relaxed state or an energized but not panicked state can be really beneficial. Especially now when everyone, including those baby sloths, has smart phones they can cue up a playlist on. So create a couple of playlists. Think about what your songs are. What's your fight song? Your personal anthem? The songs that reflect your best self? The songs that remind you that life is worth living? Have them ready to cue up when you need them.

Self-Compassion Exercises

Self-compassion is the total polar opposite of self-esteem. Self-esteem comes from the outside. Do great on a test? Great for self-esteem. Do badly? Self esteem takes a big hit.

Self-compassion means being as kind to yourself as you would be to your best friend. It is an intentional honoring of our imperfections as humans. It doesn't mean we let ourselves off the hook for things we mess up, and it's not an excuse for crap behavior. In fact, people who are self-compassionate are also more driven to be better human beings because they think they are worth the effort.

Treat yourself with kindness, understanding, and self-respect. Ask yourself, "What would I say if this was happening to my best friend?" Amazing things have happened when I have taught people self-compassion skills. The first time it happened, I was teaching a room full of therapists working on their research PhDs. One of these people also happened to already be a medical doctor. So, you know. Strong, focused, high achievers like whoa. I asked them to put their hands over their hearts and remind themselves that they experience suffering. That this suffering is part of the human condition. And to give themselves permission to be kind to themselves and forgive themselves their imperfections.

The aforementioned MD/PhD/SuperFancyPants therapist? She did the exercise and tears started to roll down her face. This person, whom I looked up to as amazing, had never slowed down long enough to give herself the same level of compassion she showed to the individuals she worked with.

Try it yourself.

> Put your hand over your heart and speak about what's really going on. Maybe just something like, "This really really hurts right now." Remind yourself that suffering is part of

humaning. Tell yourself that you are allowed
kindness and forgiveness, and that starts as an
inside job.

Mantras/Positive Self-Talk Strategies

I always felt cheesy when I tried positive self-talk, but
I also found that it worked. Think of it as talking over
that repetitive tape the amygdala is playing.

*Yes, I know you are freaking out right now. It
will pass, and you will feel better. Keep breathing.*

*You've got this. It may not feel like you do.
But your success rate for getting through serious
situations is 100 percent. You aren't about to
break your winning streak.*

*You know what sucks? This right now. You
know what helps? This isn't permanent. And you've
totally earned a cookie for dealing with this today.*

Your self-talk strategies can be put on your coping
cards if you are using them. And this is absolutely
something you can ask for help with. Let people know
which mantras you are using and have them remind
you of them when you are struggling.

Exercise

I know, I know. Crossfit and spinach smoothies are not everyone's idea of fun. But exercise releases endorphins. Short version of that? **Endorphins** have mad ninja skills ... *they block our perception of pain and enhance positive feelings* ... both of which counterbalance the stress response. Which means those superfit people who say they get a runner's high? Totally aren't lying. Freaks of nature, maybe. But totally telling the truth.

You are allowed to choose a form of exercise you can tolerate. I am not a fan of sweating and physical exertion in the name of health. But my doctor keeps telling me that reaching for a cookie does not count as a sit-up, so I gotta do *something*. I do enjoy swimming, walking, and hiking. They are way more relaxing and meditative for me than competitive team sports (but if that's your thing ... go on with your weirdo self!). Even better is when I go hiking with my bestie. We get exercise and get to chat and catch up in the process.

Find something that doesn't suck. It can be as intense or gentle as you want, but try stuff. Most places will offer a free class or free week so check those out. I had a client who fell in love with boxing by trying out a free class. It was great exercise, and it made her feel more empowered and in control of her experiences.

Get Yourself Outside

Sometimes doing anything feels like way more than you can handle. Remaining vertical is difficult enough; there certainly isn't going to be any meditation or exercise or any other woo-woo stuff.

If you can't do anything else, try to get yourself out in some sunshine. Even if it's just to sit on a bench when having a snack or something. Sunlight increases vitamin D production and serotonin. Both of which will give you a little chemical boost without having to pop a pill. It's hard to sit in the sun and feel crappy at the same time. And trust me, I've tried. I usually perk up despite myself.

If you live in a gray and gloomy place, you may want to look into getting or borrowing a personal sunlight lamp that you keep in your room. When my brother left Texas to go to college on the East Coast, he found himself battling seasonal affective disorder (SAD). He just wasn't getting enough sunlight to battle low-level blues. He was able to borrow a lamp from the campus clinic and eventually got his own. The lamp made a huge difference.

WHEN YOU'RE READY: REMEMBRANCE AND MOURNING

Once you have some good coping skills under your belt, you may be thinking about working through your story.

But the good coping skills part is really important. So many people feel forced to talk about what is going on with them without a way to feel safe in the process. It's triggering and ends up retraumatizing them.

So these techniques are things you only do when you are ready, when and if telling your story is something that is going to help you move on.

Writing or Journaling

Writing or journaling exercises, especially when taking the time to be slow and deliberate and put pen to paper, can be a good start for sharing your story. Things may come out that you didn't realize were there or that you needed to say. I am super aware that not everyone lives in a space where their privacy is respected when they do journaling. If you need to write things down to get them out and then destroy the paper, that's totally fine as well. Some ideas to get you started may include these:

- Write letters to other people. Not letters you will actually send but what you would want to tell them if you could. This may be the people who hurt you. Or it may be the people who you love but who don't understand what you are struggling with. Figuring out what you want them to know might be a good starting point for understanding your own process. And maybe starting a new conversation with them, if possible.

- Write a letter to your future self. Write about everything you went through to get to the healthiest place you are working toward in your future. List all the things you went through and how you got through them . . . as if you already have. What you come up with may surprise you.

Telling Your Story

This simply means talking about your trauma and other things that have impacted your life, as you remember and perceive them. This isn't about literal truth but the story you have been carrying with you that has affected your wiring for so long.

We talked about the brain being a storytelling brain. Creating a new story means first understanding the one we are now carrying around. Sometimes the story ends up surprising us. We don't even realize all the hateful things we are telling ourselves until it happens in our out-loud voice.

Preparing people to do this part is a big part of trauma therapy. But many people are able to do it with the help of friends, family, or other loved ones. While group therapy can be really beneficial, this probably won't be the place where you tell all the details of your story, as it can be a triggering experience for other group members. In my years of group work, we would create a title for the event (e.g., "when the rape happened"), when processing issues surrounding the event but wouldn't discuss details of the event itself during group.

The actual work of sharing the story usually starts with a trained therapist . . . because we have the skills to hold space for you and are able to sit with all the strong feelings that are coming up for you without judgment, correction, or our own experiences being triggered.

If you do want to have this conversation with a friend, family, or other loved one instead, keep in mind that the person may be going through their own stuff. Hearing your stuff may not be something they can handle, and that's totally fair. They may think they can but then realize they are getting triggered. Before you start, give them permission to stop at any point. Many times people share their stories with a therapist first and then invite the loved one in and share the story again to that person, with the therapist present to help the process.

Reframing Your Story

Telling your story in a coherent way can often help you to figure out the parts of the story that don't make sense or to see other perspectives. You may find that there was more going on than the story that has been stuck in your head. It doesn't make horrible experiences less horrible, but it can help you find meaning and work towards forgiveness.

Remember all that brain science stuff about how we have an emotional response and then we create a story to back up that response? One of the best things you can do to challenge that is to *think about how you are thinking*.

1) Think about the story you tell yourself and others. What aspects might be missing? What else needs to be included?

2) How is this a story of your survival?

3) Who are the other good guys? The caretakers and the helpers? What did they do, and how did they do it?

4) What about the things you did that you aren't proud of? In what ways were they the best decision you were able to make for yourself at the time? What did you learn from them that you can use moving forward?

Here's the magic. Brains are changing all the time . . . and we can shape that journey. Yes, trauma changes our genetic structure, but we can change it back. Life experiences reshape our DNA moment by moment, the positive ones as much as the negative ones.

GETTING BACK OUT THERE: RECONNECTION

Reconnection means reconnecting to ourselves and to the world around us. It is how we re-engage, make peace with our brains, and live the life we want again. This part can be a struggle because we are so often pushed to do this before we are ready ... before we feel safe. And clearly it doesn't work that way. When your "reconnection" is forced by others, it becomes another form of trauma ... because your power was taken away from you. Again.

You do this when YOU are ready. And yes, you may need to push yourself a bit. But now you have the grounding and coping skills to remind yourself that you are safe.

You got this.

Use Your Story to Create Meaning

The healthiest people are the ones who find meaning in chaos. The ones who are able to identify the good in situations or people even when the situation they are in is pretty awful. It doesn't make the awful things that happen any less awful, and platitudes like *"Oh, that was God's will, there was a lesson to be learned in that"* are useless. Because if God wanted me to learn something, there are far easier ways of making that happen, I'm pretty sure.

But we can learn skills of resilience and strength through the terrible things that happen. They can make us better, stronger, more compassionate, more engaged human beings.

1) **Learn from your past.** Your past is your learning experience, not the well-worn rut your brain keeps trying to live in. What have you learned that you want to carry forward? What have you learned about yourself and your capacity to survive and heal? What can you let go of so you can move on?

2) **Learn from your future.** You know where you want to go, what kind of person you want to be. Ask that person what you need to do now to get there. Ask them to share their secrets of success.

3) **Use both in your present.** Continue being aware of what and how you think. What from your past are you carrying? What from your future? What do you have to offer others as a benefit of what you have gone through? What empathy and support

can you share? How can you help others not be alone? How can you advocate for change in your community?

Finding Forgiveness

Forgiveness is serious, deep, and powerful magic. So many people think that forgiveness means forgiving those who have hurt them. And there is truth to that. But more so, I have found people really are working to forgive *themselves*. The person they are angriest at and most ashamed of is themselves. And they have been carrying the weight of that around for years.

Reminding yourself that you were doing the best you could with the information and skills you had at the time is hugely important. And remembering that the people who have hurt us are also broken and messed up is almost as important.

Thich Nhat Hanh is a well-known Vietnamese Zen monk and teacher. He is the man Martin Luther King Jr. called "an apostle of peace and nonviolence" when nominating him for the Nobel Peace Prize.

He is also a man who had a very abusive father growing up. He talks about picturing his father as a three-year-old boy, before the world reshaped him into the angry man he became. And he states that he pictures himself as a three-year-old boy, standing in front of his father. His three-year-old self smiles at his three-year-old father, who then smiles back.

He doesn't call it a forgiveness practice, but it absolutely is. Remember self-compassion from above? Compassion is integral to forgiveness. First ourselves, then others. This doesn't mean you have to be besties with anyone who has hurt you. In fact, forgiveness means you are less attached to someone emotionally, which makes setting boundaries with them much easier!

Building Relationships with Safe Boundaries

Nobody sets out to have bad relationships. But we do have a habit of picking people who feel familiar to us ... even if the familiar is because of bad boundaries. While you can't control other people, you can change how you interact with them. And a good starting point is being clear about your boundaries.

The reality may be that you may start letting people out of your life when you realize they can't deal with your new backbone. That can be a really difficult thing to process. Make sure you have healthier people around you that support your boundary work while you make this transition.

If your boundaries have been violated in the past, you may not know how to create boundaries that aren't too rigid or too permeable. Start by asking yourself the following questions:

1) Is this a person who challenges me to be my best self, or are they here because I prefer them to being alone?

2) Is being alone the same thing as being lonely? If not, how do I tell the difference, and how do I manage them as different situations?

3) Have I (or am I) communicating my boundaries effectively, or am I expecting other people to figure out what I want?

4) What are my boundaries? What are deal breakers? What is possibly negotiable? What is not an issue?

5) Have these boundaries changed over time? Do I see them maybe changing in the future?

CHAPTER 5:
GETTING PROFESSIONAL HELP: TREATMENT OPTIONS

There are lots of ways to get your brain back into shape. And a lot of them will be things you do on your own. But sometimes on your own isn't enough. If you aren't getting better, or not getting better at the rate you would like to see, it might be useful to get help with someone who has the skills, resources, training, and perspective on your situation that you don't have.

More and more, Western practitioners (like myself) are incorporating complementary, holistic treatment or referring our patients out for it. I talk about a few different options in this chapter, ranging from the more traditional treatment to the more woo-woo stuff. My intent is to show you the variety of different treatment options out there so that you can advocate for yourself during the process of healing.

For instance, other than prescription meds, a lot of treatment providers also use supplements. Not just the woo-woo nutritionists like me but even regular physicians. Some have been studied a lot more than others, like St. John's Wort for depression. So that may come up with your treatment provider, or you may want to bring it up if that's not something that your family or therapist or anyone else has discussed with you. It is super important to talk to your doctor about everything you are taking, though. Even something that seems super harmless, like turmeric, is a blood thinner that can cause other problems later if not monitored.

In this chapter, you'll read about several kinds of complementary medicine. It is called that for a reason. It is intended to use *in addition to*, not necessarily to replace. I was trained in (and am licensed in) traditional talk therapy and in clinical nutrition. But I would never suggest dumping the prescription medications that have helped people stay alive.

This is by no means even close to a complete list but some options that are most likely to be available in your area and are hopefully not over-the-top expensive. I live in a big enough city that finding services that are low-cost or no-cost is pretty doable. While I'm totally aware this isn't true everywhere, it doesn't hurt to do some browser searches and/or ask around.

TRADITIONAL TALK THERAPY

So, yeah. This is my jam. I'm a licensed professional counselor. I'm a talk therapist through and through. Talk therapy has a great capacity to heal, in support of other treatments or sometimes alone. A good therapist has the benefit of their training and a perspective on your life that you don't have because they aren't living the experiences you are living, at least at this time. They can provide insight, coaching, and interventions to help on your getting-better journey.

If you are looking for a therapist, that's going to be someone who is *licensed*. Life coaches and other certified professionals and the like can do amazing work, but likely don't have the training and resources to help you through the more intense emotional work that a therapist does. In fact, I work with a number of people with these types of certifications who partner with me to make sure someone is available if the work they do with a client triggers a trauma response that they can't handle.

If you have any choice over who you are going to see (instead of being told by a family member that an appointment has been made for you so get-in-the-car-we-are-going), it may make sense to do some research to discover who in your area specializes in the issues that you are dealing with (trauma, depression, anxiety, neurodiversity). And if you can't tell from their therapist website, it's entirely okay to ask them.

If you are going to someone who was picked for you, it's still entirely okay to advocate for what you want to focus on in sessions. Like, "My mom is really mad about my grades, and I'm not trying to dodge that topic, but I think I'm really depressed and would like to talk about that . . . and maybe the two issues are tied together." And if you feel that any therapist is a bad fit, whether one you chose or someone else chose, you can absolutely request a change. And you don't have to feel bad about that, someone can be perfectly nice, but y'all just don't vibe. And you need to feel comfortable with the person you are working with.

(Pro parent-approaching tip: If you don't like the person chosen for you, ask your parent/guardian about switching in a strategic way. As in, "I'm not trying to get out of seeing someone, and Dr. So-and-So is really nice, but I've been going for a couple months now, and I think we are pretty stuck. Can we look for someone who has a different counseling style to see if they are a better fit?")

Another thing? If you are under eighteen and desperate to be able to start therapy but your parents/adult peoples don't think you need it, and you feel really stuck? Many states have laws allowing individuals under the age of eighteen to consent to health care (and therapists, because licensed, are health care providers). For example, I practice in Texas, where the Texas Family code, Section 32.004, allows individuals under the age of eighteen to consent to their own treatment if they are on active duty, they reside apart from their parents and manage their own finances (even if the money they are managing is from their parents), they are thinking about suicide, they have concerns about drug or alcohol dependency, or they have been sexualy, physically, or emotionally abused.

A lot of issues are covered under that rule, even in a pretty conservative state so it may be worth doing some research to see what options you have on your own (or chat with your school counselor about options if you are currently in school). Do keep in mind that if your parent/guardian people find out that you are in counseling while you are still a minor, they can still request and get your treatment records, even if they weren't the ones who consented to your treatment.

ALLOPATHIC MEDS

Allopathic just means *mainstream treatment*. Western medicine. The treatment we already know about. The prescription stuff. Nothing wrong with allopathic treatment: medication saves lives. If I break my arm, I don't want someone to rub herbs on it, I want it reset and cast.

The problem? As a society, we are moving more and more towards medication as the first (and only) line of defense for managing mental illness, rather than focusing on the root causes. Anxious and depressed? We have medications for that. And rather than using them to help alleviate symptoms while doing other work on the root causes, it becomes a routine of constant medication adjustment with little other support.

This leads to over-medication, tons of side effects, and then more medications to manage the side effects. We are seeing more and more stories of people medicated to the point of toxicity.

Allopathic medicine doesn't have to be—and often shouldn't be—the endgame of your treatment. But in some cases, it helps the getting-better part happen faster. My friend Aaron is an MD (yes, a real doctor who can prescribe meds, unlike me who just talks), who uses this analogy:

> Imagine you are in a boat in the middle of the ocean, and there is a leak in the hull. You might be able to drop a pump down in the bilge and keep enough water out to make it to shore. You might be able to reach down under the water and patch the hole. But, it would probably work a lot better if you used the pump to lower the water level so you can get at the hole better. The medicine is the pump that will keep you afloat while you and the therapist patch the hole together.

Yeah, yeah. Meds help sometimes. But how? If we know that a trauma reaction changes brain chemistry, what are meds doing to help fix it? Another Dr. Aaron analogy:

> Imagine you are an Air Force base. Everything is fine, then all of a sudden all the lights go out and the radar goes dead. You aren't going to assume that just because a second ago everything was fine it still is. You are going to assume an attack.

When you have a mood disorder your radar has lost communications to the rest of the base, so it assumes an attack, all the time. We are going to reconnect communications so your threat detector, which we assume is doing its job, is talking with the threat response unit again.

Both of these analogies are brilliant, right? Medication as a tool. Medication as something potentially life-saving. Not medication as a singular cure-all. And it should never be used to control *people* instead of *symptoms*.

The more we can do to encourage the body's own ability to adapt and heal, the better. Medications can be an essential part of that journey, although they are rarely the only tools we use. Educating yourself and advocating for yourself about prescription medications will greatly increase the likelihood that they are used properly with you.

There are good quality informational portals like the Mayo Clinic, WebMD, and FamilyDoctor that can help you read more about the different types of medications for mental health issues so you can make a more informed decision about what you put in your body.

And it's entirely okay (and I'd say necessary) to ask questions about what you are being prescribed and expect real answers. Firmly but politely discuss symptoms and side effects and other concerns, and request changes when necessary. You're the one living in your body, you know it best.

NATUROPATHIC MEDS

I know, I know: "Here, chew this bark" seems pretty sketch.

Part of the reason that dietary supplements get a bad rap is because many of the ones on the market are useless. Just in 2015, the New York Attorney General tested a bunch of supplements and sent a multitude of cease-and-desist letters to herbal supplement companies based on the fact that much of what they tested had no active ingredient. And the University of Guelph in Canada studied a bunch of supplements and found many unlisted ingredients within them, many that could encourage an allergic response in someone taking them. Or they are synthetic versions of the product rather than the actual extracted herb or whole food—synthetics are generally going to have more side effects because the human body struggles to recognize them as nutrients.

So we've seen the research about the effectiveness of certain herbs and food supports. And then we feel stupid and/or ripped off when they don't work on us. I had the same experience and realized I was great about educating myself on prescription meds, but it somehow never occurred to me that I should treat supplements just as seriously!

Now I'm a huge fan of using whole food and herbal supplements in support of or, sometimes, instead of prescription medications. It is something worth talking about with your healthcare provider. Lots of Western medicine docs are getting on board, and there are lots of legit holistic practitioners out there, as well.

It is *seriously* worth seeing an herbalist, Chinese medicine practitioner, or a clinical nutrition practitioner before you start buying out your local health food store, though. There are certain supplement/prescription meds combinations you need to avoid, for instance. You don't have to purchase fancy and expensive detox protein shake kits or anything to get quality information to get you started.

OTHER COMPLEMENTARY THERAPIES

Complementary therapies are not designed to diagnose or treat conditions. They *are* designed to support the body's natural ability to heal. I love the approach of giving my body and mind what it needs to care for itself whenever possible. Many treatments can be used either alone or with Western practices (like traditional talk therapy or allopathic meds). Some of the most common, with the most research behind them, include the following:

Acupressure/Acupuncture

Acupressure and acupuncture use the same principles, but acupuncture involves using actual needles in the skin while acupressure involves tapping certain points instead of breaking the skin.

Whether tapping or using needles, it works by stimulating certain points on the body to promote healing and/or reduce pain. What is really interesting is that as we learn more about the vagus nerve system, we are seeing lots of similarities between nerve mapping and five-thousand-year-old acupuncture charts! We know that trauma reactions are a whole-body response when we look at what the limbic system (our brain's emotional response) tries to

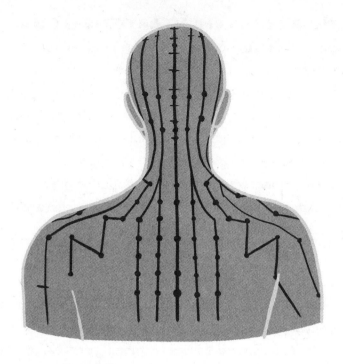

do to us, right? A lot of this response is communicated in the body through the vagus nerve I just mentioned. So there is something to all that weird needle stuff, after all!

If you are interested in a combo deal of acupressure with talk therapy, there are forms of acupressure that some therapists use, most frequently Emotional Freedom Technique (EFT), which combines acupressure and self-talk strategies. EFT is something you do yourself with guidance from the practitioner—a bonus if people touching you weirds you out—using the same main activation points an acupuncturist uses. The self-talk helps you reframe the stories your brain has been telling you while creating new ones in the process. There are a ton of free videos that walk you through the basic process, though a therapist will help you modify the scripts to work through your specific situation.

Biofeedback/Neurofeedback

Biofeedback is the electronic monitoring of all bodily functions that helps people learn to control responses that were previously automatic. **Neurofeedback** focuses specifically on brain signals, with the same intent, *to help individuals learn to manage their brain responses.* We have far more control over our body and brain responses than we realize, and both biofeedback and neurofeedback can be great ways to supplement or even speed up our healing by giving us immediate feedback when our brain and body start to get into *fight, flight, or freeze* mode. You essentially play a video game with your brain. You get set up with a Pac-Man type game or something similar, which you can only complete when you keep your brain waves in the optimal zone for your wellness. An example?

My son did neurofeedback work to help him with self-control and impulse management. Protocols were set in his game that helped him focus on that part of his brain. When winning the game, he actually felt the pressure of the blood rush to that section of his PFC. And we could even see changes in his handwriting after just a couple of treatments!

Nutrition Changes

When we are stressed we crave sugar like whoa. The brain needs glucose to maintain willpower and energy ... which is why dieting is so hard. You are deprived of the glucose you need for willpower. Typically, the more

stressed and busy we are, the worse we eat. So it's a vicious cycle and ridiculously frustrating.

Our body works best when we take care of it, eating the whole and healthy foods humans ate for centuries. Every body is different so there is no "one size fits all" eating plan. But one of the biggest issues that pretty much everyone faces is way too much ultra-processed food. And that isn't me saying give up chips. I know they're yummy. But a lot of smart researchers have found that just decreasing our ultra-processed food consumption by 30 percent makes a huge difference in how our bodies function which impacts our mental health. So like, fewer chips? And if you are really wanting something crunchy and salty, see if some almonds or cashews do the trick. Bonus: nuts keep you fuller longer, and your blood sugar is far less likely to drop and turn you into a hanger monster. And, seriously, if you can get help from a clinical nutritionist, Chinese medicine practitioner, or trained naturopath who incorporates nutritional work, it can be well worth it. I do clinical nutrition work in my practice. I have worked with many people only once or twice on diet modifications and supplements, and that's all they really needed: some basic assessments and advice to help them through the overwhelming information out there.

Nutrition and mental health really is a whole other book, but there are certain basics that can help enormously without getting into weird food-cult status.

- If we eat healthy about 85 percent of the time and enjoy treats about 15 percent, we can maintain good functioning.

- Stay away from industrial foods as much as possible. The most important thing to remember about food labels? Trying to avoid foods that have labels. The more refined and machine-processed a food is, the more likely it is for your body to not recognize it.

- Food allergies and intolerances can not only make our body feel bad, but they can make our mental health worse. If you suspect something is causing problems, cut it out of your diet. See how you feel. Add it back in. Notice a difference? Your body will totally tell you what it needs.

- Chemical sweeteners are really bad for your body. Aspartame, saccharine, sucralose? The ones that tend to come color coded in yellow, pink, and blue? Cutting calories using those is not doing you any favors in the long run. Good calorie-free sweetener options are stevia or monk fruit.

Natural Supports

These are the people who love you just because you belong to them—your family, your friends, teachers, coworkers that go above and beyond their role in your life to support you getting better. Having people who love us just because they *do* is so, so, so important to getting better. Use them! If they ask to help, let them! It takes far more strength to accept help than reject. Be strong enough to allow others into your life.

PART 2

THIS IS YOUR BRAIN ON LIFE

We are all cursed with living in interesting times. Even when we're rocking along and our lives are generally positive, they are not built for a focus on calmness, dullness, and space to think and chill. I work with so many people who just need more time in their lives to chill. No homework, no extracurriculars to impress college admissions committees, no after-school job, no cleaning up after their siblings. They aren't crazy, they are just *exhausted*.

This is an actual, real thing. We have a lot of physical illnesses, like fibromyalgia, that might be better explained as adrenal fatigue. **Adrenal fatigue** *basically means that our adrenal glands have been constantly secreting hormones to help us deal with stress, and they aren't designed to do that for days and months and years on end—they get worn out.*

While full-fledged adrenal insufficiency will show up in blood work, smaller declines in adrenal functioning won't. But it may be showing up in other ways such as exhaustion, body aches, weird skin discolorations, loss of hair, lightheadedness with low blood pressure, and more.

So yes, it is also quite likely that our continued stress response (whether trauma-induced or not) is responsible for a lot of mental health diagnoses. Depression and other mood disorders, anxiety, anger,

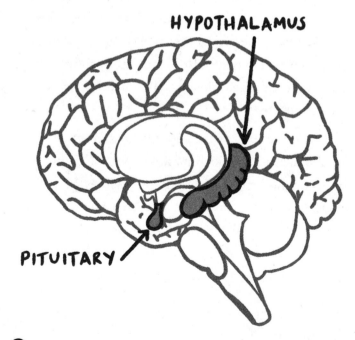

HYPOTHALAMUS

PITUITARY

and addictions can all be influenced by our stress response. And this whole stress-response system is *managed* by the brain.

The brain (specifically, the hypothalamus) is the actual master gland, the head coach. The head coach coordinates with the starting quarterback, the pituitary gland, which then calls the plays for the whole rest of the team (hey there, body). The hypothalamus and the pituitary gland control the hormonal system *and* the nervous system through their constant convos. All physical body regulation starts back in the brain.

Since less stress isn't always possible because we can't generally hide from reality, we have to focus on better stress *coping* so we can manage our business without losing our minds and trashing our bodies.

This half of the book is the part of our mission (should you choose to accept) where we start looking at the specific ways our bodies and minds deal with stress. Hang with me while I nerd out. I promise a lot of what you've been thinking, feeling, and doing is going to make epic amounts of sense.

CHAPTER 6
ANXIETY

Don't you just love dictionary definitions? Anxiety is ....*the state of being anxious.*

That's ... unhelpful.

Interestingly enough, the word "anxiety" (and its definition of "being anxious") isn't one bit modern. In fact, the word "anxious" was used more in the early nineteenth century than it has been in the early twenty-first. At least before the COVID pandemic. I've been afraid to look recently.

You know what that means? Anxiety is a classic human condition that we have been grappling with for centuries. Modern living is stressful. But modern life is not the source of human anxiety. Humanity in and of itself is an anxiety-provoking experience for so many people.

As a nerd will do, I looked up the root of the word "anxious." It's from the Latin *anxius*, which is from the Ancient Greek *anko*, which means "to choke." Well played, right?

Anxiety covers a lot of ground: It can be the experience of unease at its most chill. Distress at medium heat. Straight up panic at a full boil. It's something you feel in your body as much as it's something that controls your thoughts, which is why it can literally feel like you're choking. And it's always the most uncomfortable feeling ever. Your body is intentionally making you feel off balance so you have to attend to what it's worried about.

Anxiety is *total body chaos demanding your attention so you can correct whatever your brain is perceiving as a threat ... either a real, immediate threat or a possible one your brain is worried about.*

That right there is why anxiety is so hard to ignore. The whole point of your body producing that feeling is to demand your full attention like a naked, raging toddler running through the street in a snowstorm with a fist full of gummy bears in one hand and a bloody machete in the other.

Quite a visual right? Definitely not something you can readily disregard in the course of your day.

Anxiety demands every ounce of attention we have to give it, no matter how inconvenient the time or how unnecessary the anxiety actually was to begin with. So you can see how this relates to trauma reactions, right? It's really easy for anxiety to be our default setting if you have the kind of history that tells you to constantly be on guard.

SYMPTOMS OF ANXIETY
Thoughts and Feelings Symptoms

- Excessive worry

- Rumination (those hamster wheel thinking patterns)

- Irritability/Anger (Weird, right? Anger is the culturally allowed emotion so we substitute that one a lot for what we are really feeling. Check out the anger chapter of this book!)

- Irrational fears/specific phobias

- Stage fright/social phobias

- Hyper self-awareness/self-consciousness

- Feelings of fear

- A sense of helplessness

- Flashbacks

- Obsessive behaviors, pickiness, perfectionism

- Compulsive behaviors

- Self-doubt
- A sense that you are "losing it" or "going crazy"

Physical Body Symptoms[3]

- Trouble falling asleep or staying asleep
- Inability to rest
- Muscle tension
- Neck tension
- Chronic indigestion
- Stomach pain and/or nausea
- Racing heart
- Pulsing in the ear (feeling your heartbeat)
- Numbness or tingling in toes, feet, hands, or fingers
- Sweating

---

3 You are totally reading the physical body checklist and thinking . . . this is the same list for everything from anxiety to Ebola. Which is why so many people end up in emergency rooms thinking they are having a heart attack when they are having an anxiety attack. It's *also* the same reason many people have missed the fact that they were having a heart attack because they were also having an anxiety attack. In Mental Health First Aid training, we suggest that if you see someone with potential anxiety attack symptoms, you ask them if they know what is going on and has it happened before. If they say "no" then treat it like the potential emergency situation it may be and call 911.

- Weakness

- Shortness of breath

- Dizziness

- Chest pain

- Stomach pain

- Feeling hot and cold (feeling like having chills and fever without running a temperature)

- Shooting pains/feeling like you have had an electric shock

Of course there are tons more symptoms. These are the more common ones. A complete list of all the things you may experience with anxiety would be an entire pamphlet of list-ness. You can find lots of great lists all over the interwebz, including ones that break down all the different categories of anxiety symptoms.

Any of those hit home? You probably aren't reading this if the answer to begin with was "Nah, I'm always chill."

DO I HAVE ANXIETY OR AM I JUST ANXIOUS SOMETIMES?

You ask the most awesome questions! Like any other mental health issue, the answer lies in whether or not anxiety is controlling your life, rather than being a legit way of your body telling you to do something.

Clinically speaking, if you say it's a problem, I will agree that it's a problem. You know you the best.

Some people want a more formal way of self-check. There are a lot of anxiety assessment scales out there. The one you see quite often is the OASIS (which stands for Overall Anxiety Severity and Impairment Scale). It's well backed up by research and free to use, since it was developed by the National Institutes of Health (NIH).

OASIS doesn't have a magic cut-off number (as in: below this you are fine, above this number then BOOM, anxiety disorder). But it can be a good starting point for opening a conversation with a treatment provider or even just to reflect on your experiences.

The OASIS questions ask for you to reflect on your experiences over the past week and rate them on a scale of 0-4, with 0 being no probs, 1 being infrequent, 2 being occasional, 3 being pretty frequent, and 4 being constant companion, thanks for the reminder.

Yeah, I'm translating a bit there. You can see the entire scale with the exact wording online, download it and print it if you want. (https://tinyurl.com/k9yf4328)

The exact questions themselves are as follows:

- In the past week, how often have you felt anxious?

- In the past week, when you have felt anxious, how intense or severe was your anxiety?

- In the past week, how often did you avoid situations, places, objects, or activities because of anxiety or fear?

- In the past week, how much did your anxiety interfere with your ability to do the things you needed to do at work, at school, or at home?

- In the past week, how much has anxiety interfered with your social life and relationships?

Having an "it me!" moment? You are not alone. The Kim Foundation notes that about forty million American adults ages eighteen and older (18.1 percent of people) in a given year meet the criteria for an anxiety disorder, and 75 percent of individuals with an anxiety disorder had their first episode before age twenty-one.

SO WHERE DOES ANXIETY COME FROM?

Generally speaking, the human body works hard to maintain its chill point. So why is the body intentionally making you all bonkers with this anxiety thing? That makes as much sense as cheerfully banging your head into a brick wall, dunnit?

And once again, it all comes back to brain wiring. I am clearly a one-trick pony in that regard.

Short version: We are wired to have strong emotional responses because those responses keep us alive. Feeling anxious is absolutely an important survival skill.

Longer version: If something triggers an anxiety response, your body gets flooded with norepinephrine and cortisol. Here's what those do:

Norepinephrine is *released through your central nervous system (Hah! Nervous!) in order to prepare your body (which includes your brain) for action.* It increases your focus and attention as well as your blood flow, blood pressure, and heart rate.

Cortisol is *the classic stress hormone*. It increases blood sugar and suppresses the immune system. Many people with chronic stress also gain weight, specifically as "belly fat," due to the constant cortisol production. The important thing to know here is that when cortisol is released with its partner in crime, norepinephrine, it creates strong memory associations with certain moods to create warning signals of what you should avoid in the future.

The interesting thing here about anxiety as a stress response? The good thing? Anxiety means the body is still fighting back. This is fundamentally different from depression, which is essentially a wired response of learned helplessness, according to the work of Robert Sapolsky, a biologist who studies the stress response.

Anxiety symptoms are active coping skills in the face of threat. The problem is only when the brain has decided that most everything, most everywhere is a threat. And, boom. That right there is a trauma response.

Even once you've figured out your triggers, anxiety isn't something you can willpower your way out of. We have a strong chemical combo going on. So in the here-and-now moment of anxiety or a straight-up panic attack, you gotta do something to metabolize (process out) those chemicals. When anxiety hits, you have to face it head-on.

Any of the exercises at the end of these chapters or in Chapter 4 can be used to help manage anxiety in the moment. Give your anxiety a goofy name or persona. Carry ice to hold as a reminder. Do some deep breathing exercises.

When you aren't feeling anxious, you can work on longer-term self-training to rewire your brain.

SELF-TRAINING FOR LEARNED OPTIMISM

Like all other brain retraining, there are certain things that can really help combat chronic anxiety. It isn't a magic bullet, better-immediately-type cure, but the idea of training yourself to be optimistic has some merit behind it. There is a guy named Martin Seligman who is a legit big deal in my field. He was studying learned helplessness when he noticed that there are certain qualities that those obnoxiously cheerful Susie-Sunshine optimistic people generally have:

Permanence: Optimistic people don't dwell on bad events. Rather, they approach them only as temporary setbacks. When life throws punches, they bounce back more quickly. They also believe that good things happen for reasons that *are* permanent. Essentially, the world is fundamentally in their favor.

Pervasiveness: People who are happy monkeys tend to keep failure in its proper place. They recognize failure in one area as only belonging in *that* area, rather than meaning they are a failure at ALL THE THINGS ALL THE TIME. Sucking at basketball doesn't mean you will now make a terrible risotto. They also tend to let the things they are good at inform the rest of their lives, rather than keeping that in its own space. So, if your risotto rocks, it is an indicator that you rock. And that you should cook more often. And invite me for dinner. I love risotto.

Personalization: Our cheerful buds blame bad events on bad circumstances rather than bad selfhood but good circumstances indicate that they are good people. So basically failures are events, not people. But successes are people, not events. If you dig me?

Understanding what makes an optimist gave Seligman an idea. If we can learn *helplessness* and *pessimism*, then why can't we learn *optimism* and a *positive outlook*? Especially if we know the three big indicators we are shooting for? Interested in figuring out how to reframe your outlook?

TAKE ACTION: CHALLENGE YOUR NEGATIVE GREMLINS

Seligman created an ABCDE model designed to help you reframe your thinking as optimistic. Think about the last time you felt anxious, and write down some notes for each of these five letters:

In Seligman's model the A stands for **Adversity**. What is going down that generally triggers your anxiety response?

B stands for **Belief**. What are your beliefs about this event? Be honest, if your anxiety is triggered a lot, you are probably running a thought about the situation being awful, you not being able to fix anything, that everyone will be messed up forever, etc.

C stands for **Consequences**, meaning the consequences of the situation and the consequences of your own beliefs about it. What actually happened? And what did you notice in yourself in response?

D stands for **Disputation**. This is where you literally argue with the negative gremlins your brain is throwing down and focus your attention on a new way of coping. Remember the storytelling brain? Create a new story to use instead.

And finally, E stands for **Energization**. What was the outcome of focusing your attention on a different way of reacting? Even if you were still pretty anxious, did you handle the situation better than you may have in the past? Over time, with doing this, do you notice that your anxiety is starting to fizzle out FINALLY?

IRRITATION

FRUSTRATION

MAD

FURIOUS EXPLOSIVE RAGE

CHAPTER 7
ANGER

If you have ever looked up a definition of anger, it tends to be not very helpful ... usually a synonym rather than a definition. You read things like that and you think, "No, no ... I know what irritation is, antagonism is, rage is. They are all forms of anger. But what is anger itself?"

Well, **anger** is *an emotion designed to protect us from harm by pushing us into action.*

Boom. There we go. An operational definition of anger that is actually helpful.

Anger, like all emotions, isn't good or bad or right or wrong.

It just is.

Remember, emotions are information designed to help us make decisions that will protect us and keep us safe. They are triggered in the middle part of our brain, in our amygdala, based on the information we are processing and our memories of past situations.

Positive emotions are a type of "carry on" feedback. Our brains tell us, "Yes! Yes, all cookies! Yes, hiking with friends! Yes, funny movies! These things feel nice, let's do all these things!"

Negative emotions are the polar opposite. They are the cat scrunched up in the corner, ears flattened and growling. "No! Do not want! Does not feel good, or safe, or nice at all! Make it stop!"

Anger triggers the *fight, flight, or freeze* response I was yammering on about back in Chapter 1.

Feeling some serious anger is a normal part of being a human being. Losing control of your behavior is not. As I tell my clients . . . you are allowed to BE crazy, but you aren't allowed to ACT crazy.

Being irritated because you dropped your stuff in a chair, went to grab something to drink, then came back to find someone moved your stuff and took the chair? Totally legit. Losing it? Ruining your whole day over it? Not so helpful. Not so helpful to everyone around you, not so helpful to greater society, and . . . for purely selfish reasons . . . not so helpful to you.

When we lose our minds on a regular basis, we are wiring our brains into a constantly heightened state that eventually fries our circuits (and pushes away everyone we love in the process). We program ourselves to always be on high alert.

Our brains never get to rest and recharge, and we start struggling with many other conditions associated with this wiring change. Added up, those conditions are known as **autonomic nervous system dysfunction**. Many common health problems (heart disease, high blood pressure, food allergies) as well as many common mental health issues (depression, anxiety, PTSD) are related to a continued heightened response.

And back to anger right here, because anger is the worst offender in this regard. To borrow a famous Buddhist expression, anger is like holding onto a hot coal and expecting the person we are angry at to get burned.

The most important thing to remember about anger is that if we think we are at risk? Being threatened? We are going into brainstem fight club mode. Anger is how we prepare for that fight. The interesting part is that anger gets a lot of input from the PFC. All emotions do, obviously, but anger is pretty interesting in that the expression of it varies wildly in different cultures. Which means a lot of anger responses are taught, therefore PFC-negotiated. What's up with that?

A CULTURE OF ANGER

Why is everyone so mad all the time?

You don't have to look for a video on YouTube to see someone losing it. Just hang out at a grocery store, church parking lot, or mall food court for a little while, and you will see someone flip out over something pretty minor.

Maybe this person has been you at some point. Or someone you love. Or someone you barely tolerate but have to put up with.

There are a lot of theories about why we have all this anger, and they all make a lot of sense.

We are all of these:

- Overdistracted
- Overstimulated
- Overcrowded
- Overwhelmed by everyday life.

Wouldn't anyone lose it?

But in plenty of other countries that are just as over-everything'd, you don't see nearly the same amount of anger responses as we do in the US and Europe. One Swedish researcher was fascinated by the cultural differences and compiled a review of studies about anger, comparing anger in the US, Japan, and Sweden, and her findings were fascinating. She demonstrated that in Japan, for example, individuals are explicitly taught that there is an enormous difference between what you feel inside and how you present that to the world. It isn't something that Japanese citizens just pick up from those around them. They learn it from the actual school curriculum.

In Japan, you are taught how to handle negative emotions. Maybe someone takes something of yours without permission. You can stand up for yourself without walking up to them and punching them in the face.

But in contrast, when Americans are asked to explain uncomfortable emotions, they really have a hard time doing so. They often describe emotions as internal, not things that show up in behavior. With one interesting exception: Anger.

Anger, for some Americans, is considered a positive force of change that helps us overcome obstacles, cope with fear, and become more independent. One study found that 40 percent of individuals in the US considered their anger to have positive consequences over the long term.

That means that in the US, anger is not only acceptable at some level, it's often considered a good thing.

And our cultural rules and values about anger are getting us in some serious trouble.

- "I reached my boiling point!"

- "I was blowing off steam!"

- "I blew my stack!"

- "I was berserk!"

- "I went nuts!"

- "I unleashed my anger."

The underlying message in these symbolic explanations is that anger is in control of us, we are not in control of anger. Maybe that's why we love those movies where Liam Neeson kills everybody.

We speak of anger in a way that leads us to believe that anger is valid, it is in charge, and it must be acted upon. Our expectation is that anger requires retribution . . . and we see that our job, then, is to ensure a corrective response. And somehow, from the time we are children, that anger becomes not only permissible but a positive means of addressing situations. But, of course, it's not.

This isn't to say that anger is always bad, or always a negative force. No one has ever gained equal rights in this country by asking politely for them and having them handed over. And the energy that anger gives us can help us respond appropriately in certain situations.

If my children are in danger, my anger response will drive me to protect them. But unleashing my anger at a cashier for going on break after I finally get to the front of the line? Probably not productive for anyone involved.

ANGER IS A SECONDARY EMOTION

And you know what is also really important? This emotion that we culturally believe is driving us to success? It isn't even a primary emotion.

Which means that while anger may be the first emotion we *recognize* at some level in ourselves, and the emotion we act (or react) upon, I guarantee you it actually isn't the first thing you feel in any given situation. Anger is a secondary emotion.

The best model I have seen to explain anger uses the acronym AHEN.

AHEN is as simple a conceptualization as you can get.

- ANGER is triggered by
- Hurt
- Expectations not met
- Needs not met

Of course, it is a little more complicated than that in that we aren't usually limited to just one of these triggers but a big glob-ball of all of the above.

Here's how to use AHEN. Next time you're angry ask yourself the following questions:

1) **Am I hurt?** Did something happen here that made me feel insecure? Unsafe? Unvalued? Unworthy? Unappreciated? Just plain old sad? What about this situation is particularly nasty? Was it the person who I perceive as doing the hurting? Is it a particular situation that bothers me more than others? Has this been a problem for me in the past? Is this one of those triggers people yammer on about?

Break it down . . . why the hurt?

2) **Did I have expectations that were not met?** Was my little brain bopping along expecting a certain thing to happen, and it didn't happen? Was that a realistic expectation? (Be honest here, okay?) If it was realistic, was it life changing when it didn't happen? Someone took the parking spot you got to first. Reasonable expectation that they would follow civilized parking lot protocol? Heck yeah. Otherwise we are three inches away from complete social chaos. But is it life changing? Not so much. You find another parking spot (eventually) and get parked (eventually). Then, hopefully, you move on. So break this down next. Was it a reasonable expectation to begin with? Did the world end because it wasn't met? Some issues are for-real serious, some really aren't. Tell yourself the truth here. Is this an expectation worth getting all hurt over?

3) **Did I have needs that were not met?** This is a tough one. Because how do you define what a need really is? On a physiological level, the brain is wired to keep you alive. If something threatens the brain's

sense of equilibrium, your brain is gonna get flooded with fight-back chemicals.

MORE ON NEEDS

Certain things are going to trigger your fight response more than others. Imminent danger is a *duh*. We need to feel safe. We need to think our loved ones are safe. If your brain perceives a threat to you or your favorite people, your sweetie, your kids, your pooch? It's ON. You want to protect what's important to you! You get mad!

There are other kinds of safety needs we can't discount. Human beings are hardwired for relationships. We need the stability of relationships in order to be well. Our brains know this, even when society tells us, "You don't need anyone but your own self." Which is a really toxic message to be handing out. We live communally not because we are overcrowded but because we have to do it to survive. So with that need comes the need for emotional safety.

We need to feel secure and supported in our relationships with other people. We need to have a good idea of what to expect. We need to feel loved. We need to know that our friends aren't going to eat all our food while we make a quick trip to the bathroom. This is about our fundamental human need to feel supported by others in the world. We need to know that we are safe with the people we love, that they love us back, and that they are not going to hurt us, at least not intentionally.

We need to get out of dark alleys at 2:00 a.m. We need to get away from the person walking while looking at their phone and about to knock us over. And we also need a community of people who love us silly and make us feel secure. When that security is lost, anger becomes a really normal response.

Knowing where anger comes from is way more than half the battle. It's like 90 percent of it. How many times have you had an "Oh!" moment when you realized why you felt a certain way and then the feeling just . . . melted?

And then there is the other 10 percent of the time—it is a lot more difficult to work with.

But like we talked about above, dealing with anger is like dealing with any other piece of information that we need to take into account to resolve a situation. It isn't a good or bad thing, and it doesn't have to be the driving force of our decisions.

TAKE ACTION: WHERE DOES YOUR ANGER COME FROM?

When was the last time you were angry? When you aren't in actual imminent danger or under actual threat, and after you've used the AHEN model to break it down, evaluate the following questions:

1) What are the underlying roots of your anger? Once you figured them out, were they legit, or were they more about you and your history than about the present situation? If you aren't sure, reflect on when you first noticed that you were angry. What was going on around you ... sights, smells, noises, people? What were you doing? What were others doing? What were you thinking about? Any particular memories coming up at that time?

2) If the roots of your anger are about what is really going on in the present (versus being activated because it reminds you of something sketch from your past), then you can decide how and when you should address it. Do you have to set a boundary with someone, or is it just one of those daily

life things that just happens like losing your favorite hoodie, getting a crap grade on a test, having your order messed up but you didn't notice until you got it home?

3) If it needs to be addressed because the roots are more serious, what is the best way to do so? How do you correct the situation with as little disruption as possible? What can you do to keep from getting further hurt in the process (physically, emotionally, and mentally)? Can you keep the hurt to others minimal (physically, mentally, and emotionally)? Does it need to be addressed immediately, or can it wait until you are calmer and feel safer? Is there anyone else you can talk to who will have a healthy, supportive perspective ... a counselor, friend, mentor, family member? Someone who knows you, loves you, and will totally call you out if need be?

4) After you act (instead of react), then evaluate the results. Did it work? Is this a strategy that you can use again? Are you still angry or are you feeling better and safer now?

CHAPTER 8
ADDICTION AND UNHEALTHY BEHAVIORS

Practically everyone engages in some behavior in an unhealthy way. It could be something we recognize as biochemically addictive. We generally think of substances we ingest, but gambling is also considered a true addiction because it changes the brain in the same way.

Then there are a lot of other things that we may do that society labels as addiction, like sex, porn, food, shopping, cell phones, and more that can be very problematic for some people but aren't classified as addictions because what is going on in the brain is different, which means the treatment is also different. The one big differing point (at the time I am writing this) is around gaming (specifically video and digital games, not tabletop gaming). One diagnostic manual does list gaming as a true addiction (the ICD) and one says there isn't enough research yet (the DSM).

It may seem like a "whatever" kind of debate, but it does matter in a treatment sense. Helping someone with an addiction to opioids is way, way different than helping someone who spends hours and hours scrolling social media. But this chapter is focusing on the similarities between addictions and out-of-control behaviors, rather than the differences. Because this is a book about working through the underlying issues, and that part doesn't change.

The science-y part of addiction and out-of-control behavior and how they are different is epically complicated, though new research is starting to give us different insights than we have had in the past. We know that substance addictions set off the pleasure pathways in the brain like WHOA ... although at different levels for different people. Which helps explain why some people are more prone to substance addiction while others find that the same substances make them feel awful. Addictions are clear, especially as they progress and ramp up through time. The homeless woman with the fresh track marks over years of scars. The man who loses his home and car to gambling debts and now is hiding from dangerous creditors.

Problematic and out-of-control behaviors are less obvious in how they affect our lives and our brains. Those of us who take out a bag of chips or a tray of muffins after a tough day. Or go shoe shopping for our eighth pair of black sandals that we are never going to wear.

There are addictions and behaviors that excuse us from society altogether, those that keep us barely afloat within it, and those that become a barrier between us and the rest of the world. It's only a matter of degree, in the end.

How do we define when we cross over into addiction territory? As a relationally-trained therapist, my answer is a simple one. *When this thing we are doing (whether an addiction or out-of-control behavior) becomes our primary relationship.* Maybe not in our hearts and heads. But in our actions, definitely. When we don't have control over our addictions, we are spending time, resources, and energy on the addiction instead of the people we love. And instead of, let's face it, *ourselves.*

WHERE ADDICTIONS COME FROM

When we engage in an addiction to the point of it taking priority over our relationships with people, it's a problem. It's a coping mechanism that has moved from soothing us to controlling us completely.

Addiction is the domain of the sensitives. The empaths. The people who notice early on what is dark, hidden, and broken in society. We learn that pointing out these negatives is grounds for punishment. We are told that good kids don't notice such things. And if they do, they certainly don't talk about it. So we start taking on responsibility for everything we see that is dark and broken. We swallow it down, and it starts eating us alive. Everything must be our fault. We clearly aren't good people. Relationships aren't safe. The only way to get through is with a mechanism of coping and support.

If you have experienced trauma, if you have been hurt so badly in a way that you don't trust the world, you are far, far, far more likely to engage in behaviors that make that pain more tolerable, at least in the short term. At some point in most people's lives, we start using something to help us feel better. We are hungry for something that we aren't getting. So we start feeding that need with other stuff. Substances, behaviors, activities. Whatever we choose probably helps for a while. It soothes the raw hunger that we are feeling and helps us forget about what we really need.

In reality, addictions and out-of-control behaviors are coping skills gone wonky.

There is a huge, gray, fuzzy margin between healthy coping and problematic behaviors and addictions. It's a blurry area where we start losing control over our coping skill, and it starts controlling us and taking over more and more of our lives.

Coping skills are intended to help us stay grounded and get through difficult times. They aren't intended to replace reality or replace our real relationships. So when we can't entirely be with the people we love, when we can't entirely feel safe within ourselves, that means *whatever* we are using is no longer serving to help and protect us.

HOW WE HEAL

There are two basic categories for addiction treatments. The traditional model of addiction treatment is abstinence-based. That is, you cannot engage in the addiction at all . . . that's the only way to heal. The other is harm-reduction. This method is more of a negotiation with the addiction, finding ways to reduce the harm that is occurring in our use. Let's talk about these two kinds of treatment.

Abstinence-Based Treatment

I grew up within the framework of AA: Alcoholics Anonymous. My father is in recovery, so we spent enormous amounts of time at AA meetings, events, conferences, and having our house full of people new in their sobriety. AA was unique when it was created some eighty years ago. The idea is that people with lived experience share their support and help others on the path to getting sober.

It's a system based on giving yourself over to a Higher Power, whatever that happens to be for you. Many people who struggle with faith-based services are uncomfortable with this framework, but the AA model also can be of great benefit to healing. And Higher Power? For some people that may just be the greater community surrounding you, healthy relationships, attunement to your own authentic voice. It doesn't have to be an omnipotent God.

And you should never have to give up the medications that are keeping you sane while letting go of the addictions that sent you on the road to crazy, as some other groups believe. There are plenty of groups that honor those differences in beliefs, whether it be AA, NA, OA, DDA or any other twelve-step model program. There are meetings available online twenty-four hours a day and in most communities throughout the world. There are meetings that focus on special groups of individuals who may not be comfortable in general meetings, such as Lambda AA, which was created for LGBTQ+ individuals in recovery and the Wellbriety movement, which focuses on the specific needs of Indigenous individuals.

There are other plans outside the traditional twelve-step model that are also abstinence-based, such as SMART Recovery, Save Our Selves/Secular Organizations for Sobriety (SOS), and Women for Sobriety. These programs have also been around for some time, but focus on newer research about making sobriety effective. These programs generally also have more of a focus on the self: self-efficacy (your confidence to be able to handle what gets thrown your way) and your internal locus of control, rather than relationality or Higher Power support.

That's a simplification, but my point is that there are sober living options outside of the twelve-step model. And a variety of options mean a larger chance of finding something that makes sense for you.

Harm-Reduction

There are two times when harm-reduction treatment is the best treatment:

1) When it is what you HAVE to do.

2) When it is what you WANT to do.

So, here's the thing. Some addictions can be given up entirely and recovery can be achieved through total abstinence. One can live forever without drinking alcohol or purchasing a lottery ticket, after all.

But some behaviors are part of our daily existence, and we don't have any choice about abstinence. Soothing with food? Still gotta eat every day. Over-exercising? Getting obsessive about school or work? Using technology? These are fairly necessary parts of being human, and opting out completely isn't a realistic option for most everyone. What's more, some people do not want to let go of the substance or behavior that is enjoyable.

Some addictions are so insanely dangerous that abstinence is likely the only thing that will save your life. Meth? Not something you want to try to use in moderation.

But most abstinence-style recovery programs do not allow for a harm-reduction detox—or the use of less harmful substances to mitigate the effects of not using the harmful ones. For example, there has been enormous debate surrounding the use of methadone (legal) and marijuana (legal in some states) to support recovery from hard drugs.

Some substances require a medical detox (alcohol and heroin being the two big ones) to prevent serious medical complications or even death. Detox is not the same thing as addiction treatment and recovery. It's only meant to get you through the medically dangerous part of getting rid of the poison in your system so you can move on to treatment and recovery.

Of course, some substances are incredibly difficult to detox from even when they don't involve medical risk. Anyone who is a caffeine addict knows how bad it feels when you don't get your fix.

Straight detox (whether inpatient medical detox or chaining yourself to the bed and away from the coffee pot) can be a huge barrier for many people. For these reasons and more, harm-reduction is becoming a more frequent treatment option for many people.

There are formal, nationwide programs like Moderation Management. And there are lots of treatment professionals who use a wide variety of harm-reduction strategies in their practice as part of therapy. And yes, I am absolutely one of those treatment professionals.

Instead of thinking that you have to be completely abstinent before digging into the emotional stuff, I believe that addictive behavior is a way people manage their traumas and that we need to work on the underlying trauma and find other ways to cope with it as we are reducing the use of that coping skill. Until the addiction becomes the least helpful coping skill that someone has, it's going to be hard to treat.

RECLAIMING OUR LIVES

So here is what I ask clients to do instead.

This is clearly the world according to Dr. Faith. I am no more right or wrong than anyone else, but I have been doing this work for a very long time and have found ways of supporting recovery that work best for the individuals I work with and my own worldview/treatment style.

Use anything that works for you and dump the rest.

1. Consider addiction's rightful place in your life as being a replacement relationship.

Behaviors end up being a problem when they start becoming more important than authentic relationships with the people around us and with our own self. The substance or behavior isn't just something in our life, it becomes the most important thing in our life. Recovery is a recognition of that.

Maybe you don't feel that you have any relationships worth saving. Maybe you don't even think that YOU are worth saving. I'd beg to differ, but it's not up to me. I would suggest, gentle reader, that you give space to the possibility that there are good relationships out there to be had. And whatever you are using is never gonna love you back the way you deserve to be loved. When you are hanging out with your addiction or out-of-control behavior, consider what needs are being met and if this is really the ideal way of handling them.

Once we become conscious of our engagement with a harmful coping skill and remind ourselves we are choosing this over ourselves and over others, it becomes harder and harder to continue to make that choice. Don't step into your usage or behavior without being mindful of what you are doing. It gets harder and harder to hurt yourself and the people you love when you are doing it with intentionality and ownership.

2. You're in charge of yourself. You really are. Even if you feel that you aren't. Even if you feel that you never have been.

Ultimately, your use will change because *you want it to.* You will change because you want to be better, because you want your relationships to be better. Even if you get remanded by a court into treatment, whether or not you stay sober will ultimately be up to how badly you want to, right? No matter what people tell you to do, whether or not you do it is ultimately up to you. Remind yourself of that when you feel yourself bristling against authority. What do you want for yourself? Is what you are doing getting you there?

3. It's far easier to START doing something new than STOP doing something old.

A lot of really great clinicians are fearful of working with people with addictions or out-of-control behaviors because they think the idea is to get someone to stop doing something. I take the opposite approach, focusing on adding healthier behaviors and building healthier relationships rather than focusing on the addiction itself. We may build awareness around some of the history and/or behaviors surrounding use, but we don't generally focus on the use itself. If you build a healthier you, the problematic behaviors often become less and less needed as a coping skill. I was asked recently, *"How often does therapy consist of just getting people to get out more?"* And the answer is? A whole lot!!! You don't have to go superhealthypants, but can you add in one small thing that makes you feel better instead of worse every day? And can you pay attention to how you feel when doing THAT thing instead of the addiction thing?

4. Remember that recovery is a process.

Everything that happened to you doesn't magically go away, but hope for the future does return. You may not do everything perfectly, but if you keep fighting for yourself you will continue to make progress. This will be a lifelong journey.

5. Own your life.

You may not have had much control over your life up until this point, but consider this my permission slip for you to take it back. Accountability through and through. If you engage in a behavior you know isn't good for you, own it with honesty. Don't blame anyone else. Remind yourself that this is a choice you are making. Make it consciously. Instead of telling yourself, *"The person I'm dating broke up with me so it's their fault I'm using. I just can't handle all this,"* try this: *"The person I'm dating broke up with me and that triggered all my struggles with abandonment. I'm choosing to use because it's the coping skill that has worked best for me and trying something new feels overwhelming."* You may find it harder to hurt yourself with your addiction when you take a mindful sense of responsibility for it.

6. Figure out your triggers.

If you squeeze your eyes shut, you will continue to bump into things. If you keep your eyes open to the terrain, you can start putting together a map. When you catch yourself doing the thing, ask yourself to retrace what led to it. The HALT acronym is a big one in addiction treatment . . . am I Hungry? Angry? Lonely? Tired? If you pair awareness triggers with accountability for your actions it becomes increasingly hard to continue to hurt yourself.

7. Forgive yourself for your mistakes.

You mess up. So do I. Yaaay for being human. Have some self-compassion for that fact. Forgive yourself your failures and your human bumbling. And no, this doesn't mean you get to act terrible on purpose. In fact, if you are aware of your human frailty, and take care of yourself in the moments where you are your most fragile and off-kilter, research shows you actually take *more* responsibility and accountability for your actions.

8. And forgive others, as much as you possibly can.

I hear you. Some terrible things have happened to you. Seriously awful stuff. Awful stuff will continue to happen. Sometimes people are just toxic. Forgiveness isn't about them, it's about how much of them you want to carry around with you.

I'm guessing that's not what you want to spend your time on. Forgiveness doesn't mean allowing them to continue their toxic behavior, either. Instead, it will help you set better boundaries so you know how to better protect yourself in the future. And it will open the door to more real conversations with the people around you, instead of continuing to only converse with your demons.

9. Anticipate your continued imperfect humaning.

Do your best to do your best. But seriously. You're going to mess up. You may even relapse. And you know what? We either win or we learn. So take these experiences as new ways of getting good information about yourself. What did you do differently this time? What can you take from this experience and do differently next time? Honoring our imperfections with clarity is brave. And you have every capacity to be brave.

TAKE ACTION: WHERE CAN YOU SAY YES?

Addiction is often treated like a lack of willpower. Nancy Reagan told us it was simple enough . . . all you have to do is *just say NO*.

So that becomes our internal dialogue. Why can't we, sometimes? Why can't we just say no? It leads to a shame spiral and blocks our ability to be self-compassionate.

If addictions are replacing other relationships, that's where our first steps in healing should begin.

So sit down and make a list:

What can you say "yes" to?

Not as a replacement for your addiction. Not instead of or a giving up of something else. Life isn't a zero sum game, after all. And being told to give up the thing that has helped you the most in the past isn't fair. I know that's your end goal, of course. But we don't have to start there if you aren't ready.

Just say yes to something new. Something you used to love but don't do anymore. Something you always wanted to try.

Expand the boundaries of your life back out by adding something. What happens? What shifts? What else do you need now? What do you no longer need?

CHAPTER 9
DEPRESSION

Depression is one of those words we throw around and use as a label so casually it's lost its meaning. I've been guilty of it, and I bet you have, too. I used the word *depressed* to express how I felt when Whole Foods stopped carrying my favorite ginger cookies, even though I was really just ... grumpy.

Depression is not your team losing in overtime, misplacing your favorite watch, getting a crappy grade, or fighting with a friend. Granted all of these things have different levels of suckitude, but at their core they are all losses that cause understandable levels of grief (which is the topic of the next chapter). Grief and loss can absolutely be traumatic and can absolutely lead to depression. But with proper space and time to heal, we heal. Depression is a far more insidious problem. And sometimes it doesn't have anything to do with an identifiable loss.

Just like anxiety, depression is related to the biochemistry of stress.

Anxiety is an over-response to stress hormones. It's the body trying to go into survival mode to protect itself, based on what it thinks to be true. *Anxiety is a biochemical over-response to stress.*

Depression is the body's way of saying, "Nothing I do is going to help anyway, it all sucks no matter what." *Depression is a biochemical learned helplessness response to stress.*

Depression is also the body's way of saying, "If nothing I do makes any difference, there is no point in enjoying ANYTHING." In his book *Tribe*, Sebastian Junger writes about how depression and anger are both triggered as part of the *fight, flight, or freeze* response. If anger is preparing you to fight, then depression is your brain's way of pulling into your turtle shell . . . to not get noticed, to not be too active, to not do the things that might put you in more danger.

Depression is not the same thing as sadness, grief, coping with trauma, or coping with loss. Depression is the complete shutdown of all the things that make being human a joyful experience. If you struggle with depression, you have all kinds of feels. Guilt, shame, anger, irritability, hopelessness, overwhelming grief. But you rarely have experiences of pleasure, gratitude, connectedness, and joy. And if you do reach out for them, you feel them snatched away more often than not. Depression is the thief of all the wonderful things that make human-ing worth it. Other symptoms that are also really, really common are the following:

- Low energy/fatigue
- Low level chronic pain
- Jacked-up concentration, difficulty making decisions
- Feeling guilty and/or worthless
- Sleeping a ton, not at all, or poorly
- Feeling either super restless or really slowed down (like moving underwater or brain wrapped in cotton)
- Intrusive thoughts of death (morbid ideation) or thoughts of suicide (suicidal ideation)
- Change in eating habits (and five percent or more change in weight either up or down because of it)
- Irritability, anger, low distress tolerance

HOW DOES THE GETTING BETTER PART WORK, THEN?

The bad news is there is no magical path for healing depression. However, that's also the good news. That means you get to find the path that works best for you. And no one gets to tell you that you aren't healing correctly. Because there is no magical answer about what treatments you should seek out. The important thing is to be aware of the many options available for you to choose from . . . especially when there are people who are going to try to push their worldview about treatment on you.

Only more recently have mental health professionals started to incorporate trauma-informed care in their work. If depression = genetics + trigger, then wouldn't it make sense to look at some of the possible triggers? We've already covered all this, I know. But as a general reminder?

Very little of our genetic programming is set in stone. Of all diseases TOTAL, only 2 to 5 percent are related to a single faulty gene. However, many, many, many diseases are lurking in our DNA and can be turned on by the right conditions. The shiny-human super fancy term for this is *epigenetics*. Meaning, there is a difference between genes and how those genes express themselves in our bodies.

Whoa, wait a minute here, Doc. Does this mean that my depression that was turned on could turn back off again?

My pain-in-the-butt therapist answer is this: *That's a hard maybe.*

If you know or at least have a hardcore suspicion that your mood disorder is related to your trauma history, then it makes a ton of sense to treat the trauma along with the other symptoms.

Whoa, lady, does this mean I may not have to be on meds forever? Maybe it won't keep getting worse year after year like it has been?

More hard maybes there. Blech. I wish I knew the magical equations in that regard. I can tell you that people tend to have a way better handle on their mood disorders if we unpack the trauma. They manage present and future triggers way better. Sometimes they aren't nearly as impacted. If they are on meds, they are often able to at least decrease, or find ways of not having to increase year in, year out like they have been.

And yes, I have seen complete remission of symptoms a number of times. It is possible.

This is another one of those tough-subject topics, I realize. It's hard to be cheerful about an illness that tends to eat people alive. But like everything else, I really believe that understanding the biochemical roots of the problem is enormously helpful in feeling less trapped and crazy. You are not defined by your depression. You are not weak, and you didn't do anything wrong. You didn't deserve this. You are not being punished. You hit the perfect storm of genetics plus trigger, and now you are fighting for your life.

People struggling with depression (or any mental illness) are ANYTHING but crazy.

They are survivors, fighting back against brain chemistry that is entirely at odds with all the things that make life worth living. Those of you who are living this? Who are saying, "Hey, Depression, you don't get to win today"?

You are the bravest people I know.

Keep fighting.

ACTIVITY: WHAT I WANT BACK

Depression's fundamental difference from sadness is how much it steals from us when it strikes. It's like a police state where not just behaviors are punished but crimes of thought as well. Depression takes away our lives *and* our will for life.

Have you ever been in this place? Are you in this place now?

I would love for this to be the time that you pick up the phone and start asking for help. Help from family and friends, help from professionals. But I know how hard it is to make that call . . . and how hard it is to actually get the help you are begging for. It feels overwhelming.

I also know that if you are reading this book and have gotten this far, that's where you are headed. You are starting to get a glimmer of the thought of "I want my life back."

What do you most want back?

Of all the things that make life worth living that depression has robbed you of, **what are you missing the most right now?** It may not be the biggest thing, and that's okay. In fact, it's great because it may be easier to wrestle it away from the depression.

You don't have to do anything about this yet, unless you want to. But the intent of this exercise is to start with the *thought crime* that depression has forbidden you from having. The thought that you can do better and deserve to do better. The thought that there is a world out there that you have the right to participate in and maybe even enjoy.

Let's start right there. Write those thoughts down. Remember that world. That's the beginning of your new story.

CHAPTER 10
THE IMPORTANCE OF HONORING GRIEF

Remember how we talked about the trauma-recovery timeline? While there is no magic number associated with the time we need to heal, there's that ninety days for reestablishing balance, with the first thirty days as the most fragile and necessary part of that process. When something disrupts that experience, we are far more likely to experience long-lasting symptoms of trauma, which can look like depression, anxiety, or any number of mental illness labels.

Part of avoiding a trauma response is having the space to grieve. Grieving what hurt you. Grieving what you lost. Grieving the life that you wanted that isn't the same now.

Mental illnesses like depression and anxiety have strong genetic predispositions, but research also shows that they still require a triggering event. Unresolved grief often acts as exactly that trigger. Not having the space to heal can create actual biochemical changes in our brains.

It's also not too late, you know. It doesn't matter if it's been thirty days or years. For many people, healing an established trauma response may include going back and doing the grief work you were never allowed in the first place. Grief scares us, whether it is our own or someone else's. It feels like a freefall that is completely dark and completely bottomless.

When we don't allow or aren't allowed our grief process, this can often lead to an experience of "traumatic grief." That is a level of unresolved grief that turns into mental illness. And resolving grief starts with how we talk about it, how we support others who are grieving, and how we ensure we get the support we need in our own healing processes. In her book *How Can I Help?* June Cerza Kolf notes the statistic that the number one fear experienced by human beings is the fear of abandonment. C. S. Lewis, in his book in *A Grief Observed* stated:

"No one ever told me that grief is so much like fear."

Grief is a realization of the certainty of abandonment. It is our worst fear made reality. It makes sense, then, that we don't really talk much about grief. We fear that discussing it will somehow cause it.

WHAT IS GRIEF?

When we discuss grief, our first thought is always of death. But **grief** is *the experience of any kind of loss, any type of abandonment in our lives.* Grief can come with the loss of a job, the loss of a relationship (through any means, not just death), or the loss of a way of life we have come to know and expect.

Grief means, most simply, *deep sorrow.* The word grief comes from the old French *grever,* which means "to burden." Grief becomes a literal burden we carry, and **grieving is the process of letting go**.

Gabor Mate, in his book *In the Realm of Hungry Ghosts,* discusses how emotional pain lights up the brain the same way physical pain does. When we hurt, we literally hurt. It is just as much a bodily burden as a broken bone or serious physical illness.

That's a simple definition of grief. But grief has a habit of never actually being simple. There are different kinds of complicated grief:

- Grief can be *complex,* especially when you experience lots of losses happening close enough together to get all tied together.

- Grief can be *anticipatory*, meaning that we know it is coming so we are hurting every moment until the loss finally happens. And it doesn't hurt any less once it does happen, even if we've been grieving in anticipation.

- Grief can be *disenfranchised*, meaning that the grief is not recognized in its depth by others in our social network or larger culture. We have cultural rules for the amount of grief we are allowed to feel, don't we? A pet is considered less than a person. A neighbor less than a parent. And depending on the situation, that may not be accurate. Grief can also be disenfranchised when the relationship wasn't a healthy one. Sometimes relief is mixed in with that grief, which can in turn cause guilt. For example, the loss of a parent who was abusive is often a disenfranchised grief.

- Grief can be *delayed,* meaning that we push it aside and continue to function until the point when it comes back and knocks us sideways.

We use busyness as protection . . . until things explode.

- Grief can be *displaced,* meaning we duck and cover on the real source of our grief and have a strong reaction to something else that seems out of proportion. For example, someone may seem stoic at the loss of a parent, then weep uncontrollably after finding a dying bird in their yard some months later.

PLATITUDES PEOPLE USE THAT DON'T HELP (And My Responses)

"Time heals everything, you know?"

Yes, I know it will eventually get better. But that's not right now, is it? So stop talking.

"It's a blessing. He was in pain, he was hurting, he was ready to go."

Maybe so. But I wasn't ready. No matter how good a death it was, or how much it had been prepared for, it STILL HAPPENED.

"God never gives us more than we can handle."

God (or any Higher Power) is not busy setting up pain-and-struggle tests. Things happen to people that they can't handle all the time. That doesn't make us failures. Don't short change anyone's spiritual journey by throwing this in their face. And don't set them up to feel like they shouldn't ask for help.

"We must be strong."

Why? Why must I? Why can't I be as small, and hurting, and knocked out as I feel? Why am I not allowed my experience? Why do I have to pretend to be better than I feel? I'm not strong right now so I'm not going to pretend to be.

"You're holding up so well."

This goes with "being strong." Whether I am or not is beside the point. You have no idea of my private moments or my internal reality. And I don't want to be praised for making everyone around me more comfortable by not wailing and weeping. Because I may need to wail and weep at some point, and now I will be afraid to do so in front of you.

"I know how you feel."

Do not compare your loss to mine. Whether it was less, about the same, or worse. Just don't try to hijack my experience. Everyone's grief is unique. You may have a good idea of what I feel, but I promise you do not have the same exact experience as me.

We've all said these things, and we've all heard these things. It may not have been offensive to whomever the receiver was, but it certainly wasn't helpful. So please, bite your tongue on the platitudes. If you don't know what to say, it's totally okay to be present and be quiet.

If something stupid slips out, own it. Say, "I didn't mean to say something so stupid. I feel awkward and unhelpful, and I was trying to come up with something that would make you feel better when there isn't any magical thing to say. I'm so sorry."

Here are some things that you *can* say. None of these statements are magical emotional Neosporin. They may not help. But they won't diminish or demean the grief experience of someone else.

- You must feel as if this pain will never end.

- I'm so sorry that all this happened to you.

- This must seem like more than you can handle.

- Don't feel that you need to be strong when you are hurting and need help.

- It's okay to cry. Or be mad. Or feel numb. Anything you are feeling is okay.

- Some things just don't make sense.

- I don't have anything to say to make things better for you right now, but I will be here with you.

- I am happy to help in any way I can, but I don't need to do something for you to make myself feel better. I will offer help, but will also not do anything if that's what you prefer.

Or you can *just be quiet.* You don't have to chatter away to be a healing presence in someone's life.

Here are some more ways to care for someone who is grieving.

- Listen differently. Give people space to tell their story if they want. Don't interpret or add your own filter. Ask open-ended questions that encourage them to continue speaking if they so desire.

- Offer specific support. Don't make empty, vague offers of support. Sometimes when we are grieving we don't know what would help, but if someone offers to grab our assignment from our third period class for us, or whatever, we realize that would be wonderful.

- Ask what would help. It's also okay to say you don't know what to offer that would actually be helpful, but if there is something that would help, you would be happy to do it.

- If they say no, back off. Tell them that the offer remains open, but don't nag.

- Don't expect grieving people to be able to answer questions or make decisions. Avoid asking as much as possible when they are in the first few days of their grief experience.

- Sit with the person's pain and suffering with compassion. Do this instead of offering positive stories or trying to fix, giving advice or suggestions. Be willing to do nothing, just be with, acknowledge and honor the person, their pain and their suffering.

- Listen to their story and experience rather than telling them what you think they should experience or do.

Be aware of the bias our culture has about insisting on a happy ending. It's okay when it doesn't; it's part of being alive. And if you're the one grieving, follow this advice for yourself. Show yourself the same compassion you would your best friend.

TAKE ACTION: HONORING YOUR OWN GRIEF THROUGH CEREMONY

This is where all that stuff about the brain needing to tell stories becomes something we do with ceremony. Ceremonies aren't just weddings, or whatever, but all the ways humans observe and participate in activities that have special meaning for us. When my kids were younger, going out for burritos on Friday evenings was a ceremony. It was our special time together after a long week where we got to chill and catch up, and nobody was getting yelled at about their grades (my kids) or stressing about their job (me). Besides supporting others in their grief, we also need to respect our own. Grief is another expression of love, when you think about it. Ceremonies give us a chance to intentionally make space for that love. If you are grieving something, this can be incredibly helpful. For example, writing a letter about the grief, listening to a song that helps you process it, or creating a small altar that symbolizes your loss can all be incredibly helpful tools. I mean, go out for burritos if that sounds like a good plan. It may feel awkward to try, but you will end up getting something out of it that makes up for the weirdness of developing a DIY ceremony.

Conclusion
The New Normal

Life gets better. For serious it does. Not perfect, not pre-trauma innocence. But better. And sometimes richer and deeper for the experience of taking back your power on your own terms.

Certain things will probably trigger you. Anniversaries, life circumstances.

But your relationship with your trauma will change. It won't be the beast that controls your every move anymore.

Your trauma will be more like that neighbor with too much time on their hands. The well-meaning but really obnoxious one who pays attention to everything going on at your house and lets you know when your dog has been barking a lot or when a branch out front might fall and hurt someone . . .

You can thank them for the information, negotiate a peace deal, rather than battling them all the time. Because sometimes they give you good, useful information. You say thank you. You take the important information and act on it. And you dismiss the rest.

If you don't need to act on it, you just thank them for sharing information that is thoughtfully intended to help keep you safe.

You listen, you smile, and you think "Not helpful, Amygdala" and go back to living your life.

_____'S CRISIS SAFETY PLAN

Supportive people I trust to participate in this plan:

Situations that may trigger a crisis for me:

Personal warning signs that I may be headed for a crisis:

Thoughts	Feelings	Behaviors

What are some coping skills for when these warning signs take place?

Coping Skill	Warning Sign It Works for

What is your daily environment (school, work, activities, hang time, home)?

Any safety concerns in any of those places (weapons, substances, large stock of medications, dangerous objects, unsafe people):?

Plan to secure a safe place or avoid safety concerns:

Prescribed medications that support mental well-being:

Who helps, or can help if you ask, to manage medications safely?

What other community resources are available? What needs to be available to use them (phone/internet access, transportation, money)?

What is the plan if symptoms aren't manageable at this level or if they worsen?

IN A CRISIS, CALL 911 FOR QUICKEST RESPONSE. 911 WILL EVEN WORK ON A NON ACTIVATED CELL PHONE AS LONG AS IT IS CHARGED.

Preferred hospital:

Local crisis numbers:

Other crisis support lines (list preferred ones first or put an * by them):

Important contact numbers for me (case manager, therapist, psychiatrist, clinic, emergency contact):

Signature_____

Date_____

Witness Name_____

Signature_____ Date_____

SOURCES

Chapters One to Three
All the Brain and Trauma-Wiring Stuff

Barrett, Lisa Feldman. "Solving the Emotion Paradox: Categorization and the Experience of Emotion." Personality and Social Psychology Review 10, no. 1 (2006): 20–46. Accessed September 7, 2016. doi:10.1207/s15327957pspr1001_2. http://affective-science.org/pubs/2006/Barrett2006paradox.pdf

Beck, Aaron T. Prisoners of Hate: The Cognitive Basis of Anger, Hostility, and Violence. New York: HarperCollins Publishers, 1999.

Beck, Aaron T., John A. Rush, and Brian F. Shaw. Cognitive Therapy of Depression. 7th ed. New York: Guilford Publications, 1987.

Beck, Judith S., Aaron T. Beck, Judith V. Jordan, and Aaron Carroll. Cognitive Behavior Therapy: Basics and Beyond. 2nd ed. New York: Guilford Publications, 2011.

Beck, Judith S. and Aaron T. Beck. Cognitive Therapy for Challenging Problems: What to Do When the Basics Don't Work. New York: Guilford Publications, 2011.

Bush, G. et al. "Dorsal Anterior Cingulate Cortex: A Role in Reward-Based Decision Making. - PubMed - NCBI." 2013. Accessed September 28, 2016. https://www.ncbi.nlm.nih.gov/m/pubmed/11756669/

Case-Lo, Christine. "Autonomic Dysfunction | Definition and Patient Education." May 2011. Accessed January 6, 2016. http://www.healthline.com/health/autonomic-dysfunction.

Dean, Jeremy. "Anchoring Effect: How The Mind Is Biased by First Impressions." May 23, 2013. Accessed September 3, 2016. http://www.spring.org.uk/2013/05/the-anchoring-effect-how-the-mind-is-biased-by-first-impressions.php.

Foa, Edna B., Terence M. Keane, and Matthew J. Friedman, eds. *Effective Treatments for PTSD: Practice Guidelines from the International Society for Traumatic Stress Studies*. New York: Guilford Publications, 2004.

Foster, Jane A. *Gut Feelings: Bacteria and the Brain*. 2013 (July 1, 2013). Accessed September 2, 2016. http://www.ncbi.nlm.nih.gov/pmc/articles/PMC3788166/.

Hendy, David. *Noise: A Human History of Sound and Listening*. New York, NY, United States: HarperCollins Publishers, 2013.

Herman, Judith. *Trauma and Recovery: The Aftermath of Violence—from Domestic Abuse to Political Terror*. New York, NY: Basic Books, 1992.

Mehl-Madrona, Lewis. *Remapping Your Mind: The Neuroscience of Self-Transformation Through Story*. United States: Bear & Company, 2015.

Miller, George A. *The Magical Number Seven, Plus or Minus Two Some Limits on Our Capacity for Processing Information*. 101, no. 2 (1955): 343–52. Accessed September 3, 2016. http://www.psych.utoronto.ca/users/peterson/psy430s2001/Miller%20GA%20Magical%20Seven%20Psych%20Review%201955.pdf.

Mitchell, Jeffrey. "Critical Incident Stress Debriefing." 2008. Accessed January 4, 2016. http://www.info-trauma.org/flash/media-e/mitchellCriticalIncidentStressDebriefing.pdf.

Pessoa, Luiz. "Emotion and Cognition and the Amygdala: From 'What Is It?' to 'What's to Be Done?'" 2010. Accessed January 4, 2016. http://lce.umd.edu/publications_files/Pessoa_Neuropsychologia_2010.pdf.

Phelps, Elizabeth. "Human Emotion and Memory: Interactions of the Amygdala and Hippocampal Complex." Current Opinion in Neurobiology 14, no. 2 (2004): 198–202. Accessed May 18, 2016.

Porges, Stephen W. *The Polyvagal Theory: New Insights into Adaptive Reactions of the Autonomic Nervous System*. 76, no. Suppl 2. Accessed June 7, 2016. http://www.ncbi.nlm.nih.gov/pmc/articles/PMC3108032/.

Stevens, FL, et al. "Anterior Cingulate Cortex: Unique Role in Cognition and Emotion. - PubMed - NCBI." 2007. Accessed September 28, 2016. https://www.ncbi.nlm.nih.gov/m/pubmed/21677237/.

Tulving, Endel. *Episodic and Semantic Memory* (1972). Accessed May 18, 2016. http://alicekim.ca/EMSM72.pdf.

HJ, Markowitsch and Staniloiu A. "Amygdala in Action: Relaying Biological and Social Significance to Autobiographical Memory." PubMed—NCBI." 1985. Accessed January 4, 2016. http://www.ncbi.nlm.nih.gov/m/pubmed/20933525/.

Junger, Sebastian. *Tribe: On Homecoming and Belonging.* U.S.: Twelve, 2016.

Lehrer, Jonah. *How We Decide.* Boston: Houghton Mifflin Harcourt, 2009.

Levine, Peter A. *Waking the Tiger: Healing Trauma—The Innate Capacity to Transform Overwhelming Experiences.* Berkeley, CA: North Atlantic Books, U.S., 1997.

Levine, Peter A. and Maggie Kline. *Trauma-Proofing Your Kids: A Parents' Guide for Instilling Joy, Confidence, and Resilience.* Berkeley, CA: North Atlantic Books, U.S., 2008.

Levine, Peter A. and Maggie Kline. *Trauma Through a Child's Eyes: Awakening the Ordinary Miracle of Healing: Infancy Through Adolescence.* Berkeley, CA: North Atlantic Books, U.S., 2006.

Levine, Peter A. *In an Unspoken Voice: How the Body Releases Trauma and Restores Goodness.* Berkeley: North Atlantic Books, U.S., 2010.

Lipton, Bruce. *The Biology of Belief.* Santa Rosa, CA: Mountain of Love/Elite Books, 2005.

Marsh, Elizabeth & Roediger, Henry. "Episodic and Autobiographical Memory." 2013 Chapter. n.p., 2013. http://marshlab.psych.duke.edu/publications/Marsh&Roediger2013_Chapter.pdf

Mussweiler, Thomas, Birte Englich, and Fritz Strack. 0 Anchoring Effect. n.p., n.d. http://soco.uni-koeln.de/files/PsychPr_04.pdf.

National Center for PTSD "How Common Is PTSD? - PTSD: National Center for PTSD." August 13, 2015. Accessed January 5, 2016. http://www.ptsd.va.gov/public/PTSD-overview/basics/how-common-is-ptsd.asp.

Oxford Dictionary. Oxford University Press. s.v "habit: definition of habit in Oxford dictionary (American English) (US)." Accessed January 5, 2016. http://www.oxforddictionaries.com/us/definition/american_english/habit.

Oxford Dictionary. Oxford University Press. s.v "post-traumatic stress disorder: definition of post-traumatic stress disorder in Oxford dictionary (American English) (US)." Accessed January 5, 2016. http://

www.oxforddictionaries.com/us/definition/american_english/post-traumatic-stress-disorder.

Sapolsky, Robert M. *Why Zebras Don't Get Ulcers: An Updated Guide to Stress, Stress-Related Diseases, and Coping*. 3rd ed. New York: W.H. Freeman and Company, 1998.

Schiraldi, Glenn R. *The Post-Traumatic Stress Disorder Sourcebook: A Guide to Healing, Recovery, and Growth*. Los Angeles, CA: McGraw-Hill Professional, 2000.

Taylor, Jill Bolte. *My Stroke of Insight: A Brain Scientist's Personal Journey*. New York: Penguin Putnam, 2008.

Trafton, Anne and MIT News Office. "Music in the Brain | MIT News." December 16, 2015. Accessed September 6, 2016. http://news.mit.edu/2015/neural-population-music-brain-1216.

Treatment Innovations. "All Seeking Safety Studies—Treatment Innovations." Accessed January 4, 2016. http://www.treatment-innovations.org/evid-all-studies-ss.html

Turner, Cory. "This Is Your Brain. This Is Your Brain On Music." NPR.org. September 10, 2014. Accessed September 6, 2016. http://www.npr.org/sections/ed/2014/09/10/343681493/this-is-your-brain-this-is-your-brain-on-music.

Van Der Hart, Onno, Paul Brown, and Bessel A. Van Der Kolk. "Pierre Janet's Treatment of Post-Traumatic Stress." 2006. Accessed January 4, 2016. http://www.onnovdhart.nl/articles/treatmentptsd.pdf.

Van Der Hart, Onno, Paul Brown, and Horst, Rutger. "The Dissociation Theory of Pierre Janet." 2006. Accessed January 4, 2016. http://www.onnovdhart.nl/articles/dissociationtheory.pdf.

Van der Hart, Onno. and Friedman, Barbara "Trauma Information Pages, Articles: Van der Hart Et Al (1989)." January 1930. Accessed January 4, 2016. http://www.trauma-pages.com/a/vdhart-89.php.

Van Der Kolk, Bessel. *The Body Keeps the Score: Brain, Mind, and Body in the Healing of Trauma*. United States: Penguin Books, 2015.

Worrall, Simon. "Your Brain Is Hardwired to Snap." National Geographic News. February 7, 2016. http://news.nationalgeographic.com/2016/02/160207-brain-violence-rage-snap-science-booktalk/.

Yahya, Harun. Accessed October 3, 2016. http://m.harunyahya.com/tr/
buku/987/the-miracle-of-hormones/chapter/3689/the-two-governors-of-
our-body-the-hypothalamus-and-the-pituitary-gland.

Chapter Four
The Getting Better through Self-Care Stuff

Bass, Ellen and Louise Thornton, eds. *I Never Told Anyone: Writings by Women Survivors of Child Sexual Abuse*. Edited by Louise Thornton. New York, NY: William Morrow Paperbacks, 1991.

Bass, Ellen and Laura Davis. *The Courage to Heal: A Guide for Women Survivors of Child Sexual Abuse*. 3rd ed. New York: HarperPerennial, 1994.

Bounds, Gwendolyn. "How Handwriting Boosts the Brain." *Wall Street Journal*. October 5, 2010. http://www.wsj.com/articles/SB10001424052748
704631504575531932754922518.

Burdick, Debra E. and Debra Burdick. *Mindfulness Skills Workbook for Clinicians and Clients: 111 Tools, Techniques, Activities & Worksheets*. New York, NY, United States: Pesi Publishing and Media, 2013.

Burns, David D. *When Panic Attacks: The New, Drug-Free Anxiety Therapy That Can Change Your Life*. New York: Crown Publishing Group, 2006.

Culatta, Richard. "Script Theory." 2015. Accessed September 2, 2016. http://www.instructionaldesign.org/theories/script-theory.html.

Davis, Laura, Laura Davies, and Laura Hough. *Allies in Healing: When the Person You Love Is a Survivor of Child Sexual Abuse*. New York: William Morrow Paperbacks, 1991.

Domonell, Kristen. "Endorphins and the Truth about Runner's High." January 8, 2016. Accessed September 7, 2016. http://dailyburn.com/life/
fitness/what-are-endorphins-runners-high/.

Domonell, Kristen and Daily Burn. "Why Endorphins (and Exercise) Make You Happy." CNN.com. January 13, 2016. http://www.cnn.
com/2016/01/13/health/endorphins-exercise-cause-happiness/.

McMillen, Matt. "Benefits of Exercise to Help with Depression." 2005. Accessed September 7, 2016. http://www.m.webmd.com/depression/
features/does-exercise-help-depression.

Mazumdar, Agneeth and Jamie Flexman. "5 Brain Hacks That Give You Mind-Blowing Powers." Cracked.com. March 25, 2013. Accessed August 3, 2016. http://www.cracked.com/article_20166_5-brain-hacks-that-give-you-mind-blowing-powers_p4.html.

McMillen, Matt. "Benefits of Exercise to Help With Depression." 2005. Accessed September 7, 2016. http://www.m.webmd.com/depression/features/does-exercise-help-depression.

Greenberger, Dennis, Christine A. Padesky, and Aaron T. Beck. *Mind over Mood: Change How You Feel by Changing the Way You Think*. New York: Guilford Publications, 1995.

Prince Edward Island Rape and Sexual Assault Centre. "Grounding Techniques." 2013. Accessed January 4, 2016. http://www.peirsac.org/peirsacui/er/educational_resources10.pdf

Seligman, Martin E. P. *Learned Optimism: How to Change Your Mind and Your Life*. 2nd ed. New York, NY: Pocket Books, 1998.

Seligman, Martin E. P., and Seligman Martin. *Authentic Happiness: Using the New Positive Psychology to Realize Your Potential for Lasting Fulfillment*. New York: Simon & Schuster Adult Publishing Group, 2004.

Stahl, Bob and Elisha Goldstein. *A Mindfulness-Based Stress Reduction Workbook*. Oakland, CA: New Harbinger Publications, 2010.

Tennessee Medical Foundation. "Grounding Techniques." Accessed January 4, 2016. https://www.e-tmf.org/downloads/Grounding_Techniques.pdf

Williams, Mary Beth and Soili Poijula. *The PTSD Workbook: Simple, Effective Techniques for Overcoming Traumatic Stress Symptoms*. Oakland, CA: New Harbinger Publications, U.S., 2002.

Chapter Five
Treatment Options and The Variety of Care Available

Davis, Joseph A. "Critical Incident Stress Debriefing from a Traumatic Event." February 12, 2013. Accessed January 4, 2016. https://www.psychologytoday.com/blog/crimes-and-misdemeanors/201302/critical-incident-stress-debriefing-traumatic-event

EEGInfo.com. "What Is Neurofeedback? FAQ, Watch Video, Find a Neurofeedback Provider in Your Area, Professional Training Courses for

Clinicians." EEG Info. Accessed June 7, 2016. http://www.eeginfo.com/what-is-neurofeedback.jsp.

Gelender, Amanda. "Doctors Put Me on 40 Different Meds for Bipolar and Depression. It Almost Killed Me." *Medium*. May 31, 2016. Accessed June 7, 2016. https://medium.com/invisible-illness/doctors-put-me-on-40-different-meds-for-bipolar-and-depression-it-almost-killed-me-c5e4fbea2816#.cadpk38ga.

Korry, Elaine. "Too Many Children in Foster Care Are Getting Antipsychotic Meds." NPR. September 2, 2015. Accessed June 7, 2016. http://www.npr.org/sections/health-shots/2015/09/02/436350334/california-moves-to-stop-misuse-of-psychiatric-meds-in-foster-care.

Kubany, Edward S. and Tyler C Ralston. *Treating PTSD in Battered Women: A Step-by-Step Manual for Therapists and Counselors*. Oakland, CA: New Harbinger Publications, 2008.

Lieberman, Jeffrey A., T. Scott Stroup, Joseph P. McEvoy, Marvin S. Swartz, Robert A. Rosenheck, Diana O. Perkins, Richard S. E. Keefe, et al. "Effectiveness of Antipsychotic Drugs in Patients with Chronic Schizophrenia." New England Journal of Medicine 353, no. 12 (September 22, 2005): 1209–23. doi:10.1056/nejmoa051688.

Mayo Foundation for Medical Education and Research. "Overview - Biofeedback." Mayo Clinic, January 14, 2016. Accessed June 7, 2016. http://www.mayoclinic.org/tests-procedures/biofeedback/home/ovc-20169724.

Mitchell, Jeffery. "Critical Incident Stress Debriefing." Accessed January 4, 2016. http://www.info-trauma.org/flash/media-e/mitchellCriticalIncidentStressDebriefing.pdf

Najavits, Lisa M. *Seeking Safety: A Treatment Manual for PTSD and Substance Abuse*. New York: Guilford Publications, 2002.

New York State Office of The Attorney General. "A.G. Schneiderman Asks Major Retailers To Halt Sales Of Certain Herbal Supplements As DNA Tests Fail To Detect Plant Materials Listed On Majority Of Products Tested | Www.Ag.Ny.Gov," 1998, accessed June 7, 2016, http://www.ag.ny.gov/press-release/ag-schneiderman-asks-major-retailers-halt-sales-certain-herbal-supplements-dna-tests.

Padesky, Christine A, Dennis Greenberger, and Mark S. Schwartz. *Clinician's Guide to Mind over Mood*. 2nd ed. New York: Guilford Publications, 1995.

Pulsipher, Charlie. "Natural Vs. Synthetic Vitamins – What's the Big Difference?" January 2, 2014. Accessed June 7, 2016. https://sunwarrior. com/healthhub/natural-vs-synthetic-vitamins.

Rettner, Rachael. "Herbal Supplements Often Contain Unlisted Ingredients." Accessed June 7, 2016. http://www.livescience.com/40357-herbal-products-unlisted-ingredient.html.

Chapters Six to Ten
Specific Symptoms, Situations, and Diagnoses

Berger, Allen. *12 Stupid Things That Mess up Recovery: Avoiding Relapse Through Self-Awareness and Right Action*. United States: Hazelden Information & Educational Services, 2008.

Blair, R J R. "Considering anger from a cognitive neuroscience perspective." *Wiley Interdisciplinary Reviews. Cognitive Science* vol. 3,1 (2012): 65-74. Accessed October 3, 2016. https://www.ncbi.nlm.nih.gov/pmc/articles/PMC3260787/.

Carnes, Patrick *A Gentle Path Through the Twelve Steps: The Classic Guide for All People in the Process of Recovery*. United States: Hazelden Information & Educational Services, 1994.

Doyle, Robert and Joseph Nowinski. *Almost Alcoholic: Is My (or My Loved One's) Drinking a Problem?* New York, NY, United States: Hazelden Publishing & Educational Services, 2012.

Evans, Katie and Michael J. Sullivan. *Dual Diagnosis: Counselling the Mentally Ill Substance Abuser*. New York: Guilford Publications, 1990.

Gulz, Agneta. "Conceptions of Anger and Grief in the Japanese, Swedish, and American Cultures– the Role of Metaphor in Conceptual Processes." n.p., n.d. http://www.lucs.lu.se/LUCS/007/LUCS.007.pdf.

Hamilton, Tim and Pat Samples. *The Twelve Steps and Dual Disorders: A Framework of Recovery for Those of Us with Addiction and an Emotional or Psychiatric Illness*. United States: Hazelden Information & Educational Services, 1994.

Hazelden Publishing. *The Dual Disorders Recovery Book: Twelve Step Programme for Those of Us with Addiction and an Emotional or Psychiatric Illness*. United States: Hazelden Information & Educational Services, 1993.

Hendrickson, Edward L. *Designing, Implementing and Managing Treatment Services for Individuals with Co-Occurring Mental Health and Substance Use Disorders: Blue Prints for Action*. New York: Haworth Press, 2006.

Hahn, Thich Nhat. Anger: *Wisdom for Cooling the Flames*. United States: Riverhead Books, U.S., n.d.

Huesmann, Rowell L. "The Impact of Electronic Media Violence: Scientific Theory and Research." 41, no. 6 Suppl 1 (April 12, 2013). Accessed January 6, 2016. http://www.ncbi.nlm.nih.gov/pmc/articles/PMC2704015/.

Kubler-Ross, Elisabeth. *On Death and Dying: What the Dying Have to Teach Doctors, Nursers, Clergy and Their Own Families*. New York, NY: Simon & Schuster Adult Publishing Group, 1997.

Lakoff, George and Kovecses, Zoltan. "The Cognitive Model of Anger Inherent in American English" 1983. n.p., 2011. https://georgelakoff. files.wordpress.com/2011/04/the-cognitive-model-of-anger-inherent-in-american-english-lakoff-and-kovecses-1983.pdf

Lingford-Hughes, Ann and Nutt, David. "Neurobiology of Addiction and Implications for Treatment | The British Journal of Psychiatry." EDITORIAL 182, no. 2 (February 1, 2003): 100–197. Accessed October 3, 2016. doi:10.1192/bjp.182.2.97. http://bjp.rcpsych.org/content/182/2/97.

Maté, Gabor. *In the Realm of Hungry Ghosts: Close Encounters with Addiction*. Berkeley, CA: North Atlantic Books, 2011.

Nationmaster. "Japan Vs United States Crime Stats Compared." 2009. Accessed January 6, 2016. http://www.nationmaster.com/country-info/compare/Japan/United-States/Crime.

Zwaan, Rolf A. "Experiential Framework for Language Comprehension: The Immersed Experiencer: Toward An Embodied Theory of Language Comprehension." Learning and Motivation 44 (2003) Accessed September 1, 2016. http://old.nbu.bg/cogs/events/2004/materials/Schmalhofer/Zwaan_2003_learning&motivation.PDF.